First Trumpet—The Road to Broadway and Hollywood

First Trumpet—The Road to Broadway and Hollywood

Max Herman

Compiled and Researched by Floyd Levin
Based on Interviews with the Author

Depicting Seven Decades on the Music
Scene As a Member of the Nation's
Leading Orchestras and Later As an
Officer in the Musicians Union

VANTAGE PRESS
New York

Dedication

To my colleagues that played in the great dance bands during the '30s and '40s. They buoyed our spirits during the Depression and through the years when our troops were overseas during World War II.

I also dedicate this to the great studio musicians with whom I worked in radio, TV, and film orchestras. Although unseen by audiences, their expertise greatly underscored the humorous, emphasized the dramatic, and enhanced the romantic elements of the projects.

Contents

Preface

The first trumpet player is the band's musical leader. His intuitive interpretation of the arranger's melodic and rhythmic lines sets the mood for the entire band to follow.

Despite their vital role, first trumpet players receive little publicity and scant attention from the public. The spotlight is usually on the trumpet soloists that play the hot choruses.

First Trumpet—The Road
to Broadway and Hollywood

Chapter One
From a Rural Life to Broadway

I was born July 1, 1914 in Woodville, a farm village in North Providence, Rhode Island. The small suburb had its own mayor, town council, and volunteer fire department. My parents, Rose and Sam Herman, were Jewish immigrants from Russia; neither were musicians. My father, as a young man in Russia, was a tailor. When he came to the U.S., he wanted to own land, and became a farmer.

I have vivid memories of my grandmother, Bessie Herman. She lived with us for several years when I was a child, and I spent many hours alone with her while my parents were working. She had masterful hypnotic powers and could hypnotize a room full of people without their being aware of what was happening. I experienced her psychic talents, and I never forgot them.

This is an example of her profound ability: In addition to raising chickens, my father operated a large wood yard. During the summers, he purchased large quantities of timber from nearby farmers. He had the machinery to cut the logs and split them into firewood.

One fall, when I was about twelve years old, I was awakened by loud crackling sounds. I looked out the window, and saw hundreds of cords of wood stacked near our farmhouse—in flames! Our volunteer fire company was able to save our house by spraying it with water they

1

pumped from our pond in the backyard. Unfortunately, the large inventory of wood was destroyed and was not insured.

I was very saddened by the experience. I could not sleep at night without dreaming of those huge flames that threatened our home and our lives. My grandmother suggested that she hypnotize me to assuage my fervent distress.

She asked my father to get a newly laid egg from the henhouse. Gently moving the warm egg on my face and my head, she assured me that she was transferring my nightly vision of the dreadful flames into that egg. When she finished, she broke the egg into a glass of water. To this day, I can still see the egg that burst into flames when it hit the water! I was able to sleep very well after that incident.

On another occasion, my grandmother cured a neighbor's infected arm, which her doctors could not heal. She used the same fresh egg method, and soon the woman's arm was back to normal.

These achievements were witnessed by several family members, and while my grandmother was alive, we often discussed her miracles.

I was very young, but I understood what she could do. She explained that she was sixteen years old when she married my grandfather, Max Herman, in Russia. He was the village doctor, and often took his young wife with him when he visited patients. One of his regular trips was to Czar Nicholas II's royal palace in nearby St. Petersburg. My grandmother was befriended by a man who lived at the palace. She never mentioned his name. He was a hypnotist who claimed to have holy powers and used his skills to help the Czar and the Romanov family's problems with their dread disease, hemophilia. During my grandmother's visits, the man taught her the hypnotism that she brought with her to the U.S. about 1910. When my grandfather died in 1884, she became a very young widow with two small children, my father, Sam, and my Aunt Becky. While doing the research for this book, I investigated that period in Russian history, and I believe that the man who taught hypnotism to my grandmother was the evil monk Gregory Rasputin!

I was named after my grandfather, Max Herman. I have two brothers, Nathan and Joseph. Nate was a very good drummer in the Nick Fatool style. He worked club dates with small groups and played occasionally in klezmer bands. Although he no longer plays professionally, he still retains his membership in Local 47. His name follows mine in the Union Directory.

Brother Joe was the baby of the family. As an Air Force officer during World War II, he flew fighter planes and later commanded a big bomber. He also coached and played baseball in Air Force teams in Europe.

Joe was a switch hitter and a very fast runner. During one important game, he hit a winning home run while batting right handed. The next day, his homer also won the game. That time he batted with his left hand!

He was one of the few fielders who played shallow and could catch balls over his shoulder that were hit deep into the outfield. Joe retired as Lt. Colonel and lives in Orlando, Florida.

Most of my friends' parents came from various European countries and settled in North Providence. Some were farmers, carpenters, mechanics, tailors, shoemakers, and merchants. They all worked hard to raise and educate their families. Despite our diverse backgrounds and religions, we got along without any antagonism or discrimination.

I attended a four-room country school that taught from

the first through the eighth grade. Music was included daily in all classes. I started taking trumpet lessons at age eight from Alexander Billincoff, an outstanding teacher, although he was only eighteen years old. To this day, I marvel at his great knowledge and the many things he taught me.

During the warm summer evenings, I often practiced on the back porch. The sound of my horn could be heard on adjacent farms. Our friends the Morrisseys would call requesting "When Irish Eyes Are Smiling," which they enjoyed hearing a mile away.

Cornetist Bobby Hackett and I were approximately the same age. We were fourteen or fifteen years old when we played a job for one of the volunteer fire companies in the local area at their annual carnival. They always had a four or five-piece band playing dime-a-dance sets to raise money.

Bobby Hackett played banjo and ukulele and I played trumpet along with a drummer and piano player. Bobby was a natural phenomenon; he had no formal training, but played great jazz fiddle, banjo, and cornet.

He loved the cornet and soon began playing the tender tones that later made him a major star. After working in local bands, he worked in a trio with Pee Wee Russell in Boston in the '30s, led his own band in 1936, moved to New York, worked with Joe Marsala on 52nd Street, and came to prominence playing the Bix Beiderbecke role at Benny Goodman's famous Carnegie Hall concert in January 1938.

Bobby always played with restrained elegance and sensitivity, and his lovely improvisational journeys never veered far from the melody. He was featured on many wonderful LPs Jackie Gleason made with a full orchestra.

Bobby was only 61 when he died in 1976—and he will always be missed.

Nick Fatool was a great drummer, and a good friend. He was also about the same age as Bobby Hackett, and, as youngsters, we all played together in many bands in the Providence area. Nick always had an ambition to play with Benny Goodman, and Bob Crosby was my goal. As you will note, we both eventually achieved our objectives.

When I was thirteen years old, I was hired to play first trumpet with Perry Borrelli's Orchestra, the area's leading dance band.

There was no high school in Woodville, so I attended Hope High School in nearby Providence, and our town paid the tuition. Since I was an accomplished musician when I reached Hope High, I became the principal trumpet player in the school's band and orchestra.

While in high school, I formed my own band that played weddings, bar mitzvahs, and other events. We also played in several local restaurants and nightclubs that featured "live music" at that time.

I was about twenty years old when I organized and managed the town baseball team, the "Woodville Townies," in a local league in 1933 and 1934.

As a youthful prank, I wired Senator Jessie Metcalf for financial assistance for our ball team. He sent a check for ten dollars! (We only netted $8.50, the telegram cost $1.50.)

My brother Nate played on my team when he was about fifteen or sixteen years old. He was a great catcher and outfielder and had a powerful arm; his batting average was over 300. During one of our all-star games, he hit a home run in the bottom of the ninth inning to win the game. My younger brother, Joe, was the "Townies" bat boy.

I produced small amateur musical shows and barn

dances to raise money for the ball team and the Fire Department.

I was known as "Max, the Booker" because I made sure that every girl who wanted to attend my barn dances was escorted by a ball player, their date for the evening. Romances often developed and several marriages were the result of my "date service."

A young Providence musician, Al Antonelli, was a good friend and ranks among the best pianists and arrangers with whom I have ever worked. We frequently attended afternoon movies together. It took a while for me to understand a situation that usually occurred during the films.

When we entered the theater, Al was always sober, but when we left, he appeared to be drunk. I finally realized that he had a pint of liquor in his inside coat pocket and frequently sipped from the straw in the bottle. Al died at a very young age—I wonder why?

After graduating from high school, one of my first jobs was at a local Chinese restaurant, the Port Arthur, playing dance music for lunch and dinner patrons. I was quite smug about my ability. After each evening session, I would leave my trumpet on my chair, and at the next performance, I would always play without warming-up.

One day, some of the musicians filled my horn with water. I got on the stand just as the bandleader gave the downbeat for the opening number. My first note expelled a stream of water that drenched the leader. After that embarrassing incident, I always warmed-up before each job!

I played in the local big bands, at ballrooms and theaters. After a brief period with Clint Noble's orchestra in 1934 at the local Biltmore Hotel, I went with them to Columbus, Ohio, where I met a fine local trumpet player, Abe Dworkin. Our paths would cross again later.

One of my earlier jobs was playing in a pit orchestra at

a theater that catered to the Italian community. Troops of Italian entertainers appeared at the theater and many brought their music for us to accompany them. The trumpet parts on their Italian music were usually written for "F," "A," or "C" horns. We played "B Flat" trumpets. Thanks to my fine teacher, Alexander Billincoff, I had no trouble transposing those parts to play on my "B Flat" horn.

Before leaving Woodville, I also successfully managed the election campaigns for the mayor and several other town officials.

Chapter Two
A Young Man with a Horn on His Way to the Great White Way

The Joe Haymes Orchestra

In the summer of 1936, I went to New York hoping to become part of the Golden Era of the Big Bands. Shortly after I arrived, I was very thrilled to visit the Kate Smith Radio Show and hear Jack Miller's super trumpet section that included Mannie Klein, Charlie Margolis, and Charlie Spivak.

I heard that Joe Haymes, leader of one of the era's best bands, was looking for a first trumpet player. Haymes had recently re-formed his band after his previous successful group was taken over by Tommy Dorsey after he quit as co-leader of the Dorsey Brothers Orchestra.

When I learned that Haymes would be at a rehearsal studio on Broadway and Seventh Avenue, I walked into the studio and told him that I was a first trumpet player. He immediately asked me to sit-in, and after playing a few arrangements, he offered me the job. I replaced the great Zeke Zarchy, who was leaving to join Benny Goodman's orchestra.

Haymes was a super arranger, and by playing his arrangements, many of us young musicians learned how big bands were structured. He had a recording contract with

American Record Corporation, and, with this band, on August 13, 1936, I proudly made my first recordings.

My hometown buddy, Nick Fatool, joined the Joe Haymes orchestra in New York about a year later, and I enjoyed working with him again.

I remember a humorous incident when we played for the Carnegie family in Pittsburgh. They provided lots of food and drinks. Cappy Lewis, who played trombone in the Haymes band, had a few too many drinks and admired a beautiful silver coffee pot and thought it would be a good gift for his wife. Between musical sets, he put the pot under his coat, and walked across the dance floor in front of tables where guests were dining. As he approached the middle of the dance floor, the pot fell out of his coat. Cappy looked around, and said, "Who threw that?"

Mike Michaels was an outstanding trombone player in the Haymes band but he had a serious drinking problem. At rehearsals he would play wonderfully, and assured Joe Haymes that he would not drink before the job. It seldom happened. He frequently got drunk before the performances and couldn't play at all.

Our leader, Joe Haymes, was one of the most talented arrangers in the business—but he, too, enjoyed his liquor. Occasionally, when he was late for our first set, we would start without him. Once, during an engagement in a Pennsylvania mining town, Joe arrived late and a little "tipsy." The ballroom doorman, thinking he was a drunken patron, refused to admit him. When he tried to convince the man that he was the leader of the band, a pair of brawny "bouncers" appeared and threw him out! He eventually arrived on the bandstand a little shaken by the experience.

The band played many engagements in small towns not far from New York City. The band manager, Dick Gabbe, traveled with us in Joe Haymes' car that I drove. He was later a partner in the Gabbe, Lutz, and Heller Agency that represented Lawrence Welk, Frankie Laine, and other top stars.

Dick was a spokesman for the band and cleverly handled any problems that occurred on the road. He was the first of the great "double-talkers." He spoke with great authority, but was never really understood. Somehow, he always managed to quickly resolve any unforeseen difficulties.

On New Year's Eve in 1936, publisher William Randolph Hearst hired the Joe Haymes band to entertain guests at his mansion on Riverside Drive in New York City. This was a very large party, and there was food and liquor for us. Between sets, a couple of the musicians, having imbibed considerably, got into a serious argument. They agreed to settle the dispute outside after the job.

At 3:00 A.M. on New Year's Day, in front of the Hearst Mansion, the two musicians started to fight while the rest of the band cheered them on. I thought this was ridiculous and stepped between them to halt the battle. Mike Michaels decided to help me and used his trombone case to separate the combatants. The trombone came flying out the case, and hit me in the head!

I was popular with all the musicians and they were concerned about my injury. Mike's trombone was not damaged. The fight never resumed, and everybody went home. The two fighters were unharmed, but I awoke the next day with a large lump on my forehead.

I am happy to say I have never been drunk in my life, although I have always enjoyed moderately drinking occasionally—perhaps that is why I have outlived so many of my colleagues.

Glenn Miller came to hear us during Joe Haymes' 1938 engagement at the Roseland Ballroom in New York City. He complimented me on my trumpet work saying, "Max, you sure batted them out!"

Glenn was re-forming his band and was looking for musicians. He asked me if I knew a good clarinet player. I had recently attended a rehearsal of a new band being formed by my friend from Providence, Lew Sherwood, trumpet player with the Eddie Duchin orchestra.

I was very impressed with a young clarinetist in the band, and recommended him to Glenn, who hired Wilbur "Willie" Schwartz immediately to replace departing lead clarinetist Irving Fazola. For many years, "Willie's" wonderful tone contributed to the unique sound of the band's reed section. None of the many Miller imitators could ever duplicate that exceptional quality originally arranged by Dave Rose.

Although Joe Haymes led one of the best bands in the country, curiously, he often did not have steady jobs. I had a good reputation in New York as a first trumpet player, so I was often offered short engagements with other bands—but I always returned to Joe.

Some of the bands I played and recorded with during that period were led by Will Hudson and Eddie DeLange, Nat Brandwynne, George Hall, Larry Clinton, Wingy Manone, Bunny Berigan, Gus Arnheim, Jesse Crawford, and Happy Felton.

The Hudson-DeLange Orchestra was one of the gentlest and most successful swing bands during the mid-'30s. The co-leaders composed many wonderful songs including "Darn That Dream," "Do You Know What It Means to Miss New Orleans?," "Moonglow," "White Heat," "Jazznocracy," "Organ Grinder's Swing," etc.

"Organ Grinder's Swing," with Mitchell Parish's lyrics, was Will Hudson's big hit, and the dancers requested it during every performance. (Incidentally, just a few months earlier, right after I joined Joe Haymes' band, Hudson's hit was the first tune I ever recorded.)

Hudson, who also did the arranging, had previously written for Fletcher Henderson, Cab Calloway, Don Redman, Louis Armstrong, Earl Hines, and Ina Ray Hutton. He later arranged for Glenn Miller's Army Air Forces Band during the war, and Eddie DeLange became a songwriter for Hollywood films.

Nat Brandwynne led a fine society orchestra featuring his light and tasteful piano work. I spent a few pleasant months with him in hotel jobs as the only brass player in the band. Nat was not a jazzman, but he retained the respect and admiration of his fellow musicians and eventually conducted the house band at Las Vegas' Caesar's Palace Hotel.

George Hall had a great following because of his radio broadcasts from the Grill Room at the Taft Hotel in New York for eight consecutive seasons. When he hired me for a recording session, he asked his first trumpet man to play second, and gave me the first part. Evidently he was pleased with my playing and called me into the control room after the session. He wanted me to join his band and had bookings on the road and steady engagements for about a year. This was not my style of band, so I quoted a price I knew he would turn down.

To my surprise, he accepted my price, and asked me to institute changes that would upgrade his band that already included Johnny Guarnieri, Tony Mottola, and George Paxton. Some of the musicians I recruited for Hall were Nick Fatool on drums, Doc Goldberg, from the Hudson-DeLange band, on bass, and Eddie Kolyer on trombone. With this augmented group of fine players, the band greatly improved, and I enjoyed working with them. The next year was one of my best periods in the music business thus far.

George Hall's star vocalist, Dolly Dawn, made some recordings of her own while still with the band and hired me as first trumpeter on her initial Dawn Patrol recordings.

After the Hall band broke up, Tony Mottola went with Frank Sinatra; Nick Fatool fulfilled his dream to play with Benny Goodman; Doc Goldberg joined the Glenn Miller orchestra; George Paxton took over as Ina Ray Hutton's star saxman and arranger; Johnny Guarnieri and Eddie Kolyer went into the New York studios.

On September 2, 1938, I played on Lee Brown's first date for Bluebird Records, a subsidiary of RCA Victor. Since I was the record firm's "house" first trumpet player, and Brown's band was unknown at the time, the producer insisted that I play first trumpet to assure a good sound on their four numbers.

Wingy Manone, the famous one-armed New Orleans trumpet star, was a great showman and a crowd pleaser. He usually worked with a small jazz group. Occasionally, when he had a job for a big band, he would hire me to play first trumpet. Since he did not have much range as a trumpet player, I got the job only if I agreed to augment his energetic closing notes.

Wingy masterfully created a dramatic illusion of ending on a high note. To achieve this pretense, he would start down low, and, with "body English," pretended to be making a great effort as he gradually ascended upward. Although he finally ended in the middle register, he always received a great ovation from the audience as I blew the high note ending that the audience thought he was playing.

I worked only one night with Bunny Berigan's band at the Paradise Restaurant on Broadway—but it was a memorable occasion. At that time, many large restaurants had big stage shows every night. Since the union contracts called for double scale on the seventh day, relief bands were often hired to back the shows on Sunday. One week, when Berigan conducted the show and played a featured spot with his band, I substituted for his first trumpet player.

He had recently recorded his popular "I Can't Get Started," and it was being played on the radio every day. He had many requests for the Vernon Duke tune that was introduced by Bob Hope in the Ziegfeld Follies just a year before.

I enjoyed hearing his powerful solos. Berigan was influenced by Louis Armstrong, and had a broad range, a fine harmonic sense, and played in a unique uninhibited fashion. Unfortunately, he was only 34 years old when he died a few years later.

Gus Arnheim led the top West Coast band during the pre-swing era. Bing Crosby was his vocalist during their lengthy stay at Los Angeles' Cocoanut Grove at the Ambassador Hotel. In 1937, when Arnheim revamped and updated his orchestra, he toured the mid-West and East. He needed a first trumpet player for his six-week engagement at the New Yorker Hotel in Manhattan. Charlie Spivak recommended me, and I played in the band during the hotel date and a few weeks of one-nighters that followed.

Arnheim was leading a well-rehearsed, hard-driving, Goodman-like band. We played some fresh arrangements that featured his powerful brass section. Those arrangements were written by our very tall young pianist. His name was Stan Kenton. Our drummer was Lou Singer, who later became the busiest studio percussionist in Hollywood.

Jesse Crawford was one of the most popular organists of all time. He had a prestigious job at New York's Paramount Theater during the '30s. When he took some time off to lead a society band for a few weeks at one of the local hotels, he asked me to play first trumpet. The Joe Haymes band was "between jobs," and I was glad to get the gig.

Happy Felton spread his girth and cheer leading an entertaining orchestra that featured a very young trumpeter, Shorty Solomon, and a fine jazz violinist, Armand Camgros. During Happy's humorous antics, it was difficult to stifle my laughter while trying to blow my horn. He was a very funny man. Felton later gained fame with his Brooklyn Dodger's "Knot Hole Gang."

After some short tours with Larry Clinton, and another stint with my favorite, Joe Haymes, my dream came true. It was three years after I left Rhode Island—when I got the call from Bob Crosby!

Chapter Three
Three Years with the Bob Crosby Band

"Now, with Max Herman [in our trumpet section] the feeling and precision of our brass is attaining a new degree of perfection."

Bob Crosby, *Down Beat* magazine, June 1940

I joined the Bob Crosby band on October 3, 1939 at the World's Fair in New York City. I sat down in the first trumpet chair and played my initial date with the band—without a rehearsal!

Their commitment to jazz's traditional tunes was evident in their sensitive arrangements of such classics as "High Society," "Muskrat Ramble," "Wolverine Blues," "Original Dixieland One-Step," etc. During the "Swing" era, no other orchestra sustained the sounds of early New Orleans and Chicago-style jazz as authentically and as successfully.

Less than three weeks after I joined, on October 23, I made the first of many recordings with them. What a thrill! My boyhood fantasy had become a reality! During that memorable record date, we recorded Bob Haggart's arrangement of Sy Oliver's "For Dancers Only," a number requested almost every night for the next several years!

The ex-Goodman pianist Jess Stacy, replacing Joe Sullivan, joined the same day. Sullivan had previously left the band in 1937 suffering from tuberculosis and Bob Zurke came aboard. A few months later, when the band was playing at the Hotel Congress in Chicago, they staged a huge benefit to raise funds for Sullivan's medical expenses. After a stint in a TB sanatorium, he returned and stayed with the band until Stacy took over the piano stool.

I was recommended for the job by Zeke Zarchy who was leaving Crosby to join Red Norvo's orchestra. Zeke, who also preceded me in the Joe Haymes band, replaced Charlie Spivak a year before in Crosby's trumpet section. Charlie was leaving to join Tommy Dorsey briefly and then to play in Jack Teagarden's orchestra before launching his own successful group with Nelson Riddle writing his arrangements.

During that era, musicians changed jobs frequently as bandleaders strived to improve the quality of their orchestras. For example, Zeke Zarchy left Joe Haymes to join Benny Goodman in '36, and later that year, he went with Artie Shaw. For the next two years, he played with Bob Crosby, Red Norvo, and Tommy Dorsey. He returned to Crosby briefly before becoming a member of Glenn Miller's orchestra in '39!

Charlie Spivak was my idol as a first trumpet player. He played ballads with a sound you would never forget. Gil Rodin, the manager of the Bob Crosby band, was concerned about whether I could play their theme song, "Summertime," in the same style and sound as Charlie Spivak. In 1937, when he joined the trumpet section, he elevated "Summertime" to a lofty level with his great breath control and tender feeling.

Charlie, confirming Zeke Zarchy's strong recommendation, told Rodin, "I have heard that kid playing with Joe Haymes, and he can do the job!"

"Summertime" was the opening lullaby in George

Gershwin's *Porgy and Bess*. The folk opera opened in New York shortly after members of the disbanded Ben Pollack orchestra incorporated to form their own band. They hired the Dorsey Brothers' vocalist, Bob Crosby, Bing Crosby's young brother, to front them. Bob became a very good leader. He had a delightful sense of humor and handled the audiences very well.

Dean Kincaide's lovely arrangement of "Summertime" for Crosby included a beautiful trumpet solo originally played by Andy Ferretti and later recorded with the band by Billy Butterfield. Often we had to play several consecutive choruses at a very slow tempo. The difficult trumpet solo required each note to be sustained. After I inherited that challenging role, I played the solo every night for the next three years!

When you hear "Summertime," it is usually sung by a disciplined soprano. Very few of the great modern trumpet players risk it. The superstar Louis Armstrong knew what it required, and he often complimented me for playing the number night after night.

I was soon given the nickname, "Pontiac," by the bandmembers when a photo of me appeared in Selmer's 1940 *Down Beat* ad. Because of my prominent nose, they thought I resembled the Indian chief on the Pontiac hood ornament, and from then on, I was called "Pontiac."

One night, as a prank, my good friends, Muggsy Spanier and Al King, the other two trumpet players in the band, tampered with my horn before we began.

I had to play an entire set with a strange mouthpiece covered with garlic! It reminded me of the similar escapade that occurred years before at the Chinese restaurant in Providence, when I showered the bandleader with water.

When Muggsy Spanier joined us, he was already famous for his great sixteen Decca recordings with his Ragtime Band that re-defined the small band Dixieland sound. His presence attracted large audiences wherever we appeared. He stayed with us for only about eight months, but we all enjoyed working with him.

Muggsy was replaced by Bob Goodrich in January 1941. Bob, who never became well-known, was a wonderful section player and worked well with the Bob Cats. He could have been one of the best jazz players in the big band era if he had more power and endurance.

In September, Goodrich was replaced by Yank Lawson, one of the band's founding members who returned after a hiatus. At the same time, Lyman Vunk joined our trumpet section. He was a powerful player with a great high range. Since he was more versed in the modern style, he played lead trumpet on some screaming arrangements Phil Moore wrote for the band. The arrangements were not in the style that made the Bob Crosby band famous.

For two consecutive years, the Bob Crosby band returned to the Catalina Island Casino Ballroom to play six-week engagements. We also made dozens of recordings for Decca, including a few with Fred Astaire and Bing Crosby. We continued working college dates, ballrooms, and one-nighters on the West Coast during the early war years.

The Crosby band appeared on many radio programs. One of them was at NBC in Hollywood. After one of the broadcasts, I was walking out of the studio and the band manager Gil Rodin called to me. He was talking to Artie Shaw, and Artie wanted to know who was playing first trumpet. Gil introduced us and Artie said, "You sure played great, Max!" I was very flattered for praise from such a fine artist as Artie Shaw. Applause and compliments are important for people in any industry.

Members of the Bob Crosby Orchestra

Metronome magazine's great columnist, George T. Simon, helped organize Glenn Miller's first orchestra and played drums with the band. In his highly acclaimed book "The Big Bands" (Macmillan 1967), Simon astutely wrote, "The Bob Crosby band had a purpose of thought, both musical and otherwise, plus a sense of freedom and playing—all combined with an air of maturity—that you won't find in any other orchestra."

Each of the following nineteen Crosby band members played an important role in the history of jazz, and I am proud to have been associated with them. As this is written, only Doris Day, Ernani Bernardi, Zeke Zarchy, Buddy Morrow, and "Doc" Rando are still alive.

Ray Bauduc and Bob Haggart had already introduced and recorded their famous drums/bass duet "Big Noise From Winnetka" when I joined the band. It was a huge success, and they had to play it every night—sometimes several times! They were both in the band since its inception and kept the orchestra and the Bob Cats swinging. Their great composition "South Rampart Street Parade," recorded by the Crosby band in 1937, is still one of the world's most popular Dixieland standards.

Bauduc's drumming was innovative, imaginative, and exciting. His syncopated fills and clean, technically precise accompaniment patterns set the standard for Dixieland drumming. Haggart's brilliant arrangements enabled the Crosby band to retain its original unique style and thrust. Bob Crosby described him as "the undiscovered George Gershwin of our day." In addition to "Big Noise" and "South Rampart Street Parade," Haggart wrote several fine numbers recorded by the band including "I'm Prayin'

Humble" and "I'm Free," which, with lyrics by Johnny Burke, became "What's New?" one of his biggest hits.

Ernani Bernardi was a very active participant in the Big Band era and an early member of the Bob Crosby orchestra. As an outstanding alto saxophonist, clarinetist, and arranger, he also played and recorded with orchestras led by Joe Haymes, Joe Venuti, Bob Zurke, Toots Mondello, Benny Goodman, Ziggy Elman, Jimmy Dorsey, Tommy Dorsey, Raymond Scott, Kay Kyser, and more. (Tommy Dorsey's famous theme, "Getting Sentimental Over You" and the Benny Goodman hit "And the Angels Sing" were both arranged by Bernardi.)

He was known simply as "Noni," and became a very successful builder-contractor in the San Fernando Valley after World War II. He did such great work for the community, that many of his patrons urged him to run for a chair in the Los Angeles City Council.

I suggested that he hire a large flatbed truck, and decorate it with signs reading "Get On The Bernardi Band Wagon." I recruited a group of musicians including former Bob Crosby band members, and we played jazz on the truck at the shopping center in Noni's district where he addressed the shoppers.

He easily won the election! My wife, Ida, and I still live in the last home he built before taking office.

After a long musical career, and a second vocation as a builder of quality homes, Noni became very active in local politics. He diligently criticized excessive spending measures, and fought against waste and corruption. He was always a staunch defender of the taxpayers' money and vigorous champion of his constituents. He was the longest serving member of the Los Angeles City Council when he retired in 1993 after serving for thirty-two years.

Shortly after his retirement from city government, he arranged and produced an all-star video, "The Way It Was," featuring seventeen veterans of the swing era. The video is now a nostalgic tribute to several great participating musicians who since have passed away.

As a result of the Los Angeles City Council's vote, a large plaza in the Van Nuys Civic Center now bears the name "Ernani Bernardi Plaza," and a Multipurpose Senior Center in Van Nuys is named in his honor.

Billy Butterfield, a great trumpet soloist in the Bob Crosby orchestra, was also featured with the Bob Cats. I feel that Billy was the best all-around trumpet player during the big band era. He could lead, and play great solos like the unforgettable "Stardust" he later recorded with Artie Shaw. The key word for Billy was "taste."

He had an intuitive approach to each number which he played with great sensitivity. Like every trumpet player, his teeth were very important. His two front teeth had been extracted and an artificial pair was cemented in place to support his mouthpiece. Without them, he was unable to blow his horn.

Unfortunately, the teeth fell out during a weekend while we were playing a theater engagement in the early '40s. There was a frantic search Sunday morning for a local dentist to make some emergency repairs. Fortunately, the theater manager located a dentist who replaced Billy's teeth in time for the matinee.

In the '60s, Billy was featured in the successful World's Greatest Jazz Band, co-led by ex-Crosby members, Bob Haggart and Yank Lawson.

Ray Conniff was a fine arranger and trombone player in the band. He played in Bunny Berigan's orchestra before joining us. In later years, he successfully assembled a group of singers and instrumentalists that performed his arrangements of light popular music and became internationally famous with many hit records.

Ray and I were roommates during the Crosby band's one-week stand in Cedar Point, Ohio, where I met my future wife Ida earlier when I was playing with the Eddie DeLange orchestra.

Doris Day (her real name was Doris Kappelhof) was only about seventeen years old when she was hired during our engagement at a theater in Cincinnati, her hometown. Bob Crosby and Gil Rodin auditioned several singers—and she got the job.

She had previously sung with local bands led by Jimmy James and Barney Rapp, but this was her first major opportunity. The June 1940 issue of *Down Beat* magazine published Doris' photo in an article that said she was hired to succeed Marion Mann as "fem thrush with the Dixie band."

Doris had a good voice, but this was her first important position, and Crosby needed a vocalist with more stage experience, so she remained in the band only a short time. I do not think she appeared on any of our recordings. She was replaced by Bonnie King and soon followed by Liz Tilton and Johnny Desmond. Later, Doris' hit recording of "Sentimental Journey" with Les Brown's orchestra rapidly accelerated her career, and she became a major film star. We remained friends, but our paths have not crossed for many years.

Irving Fazola brought an authentic New Orleans feeling to the band along with his fellow Crescent City colleagues: Ray Bauduc, Eddie Miller, Nappy Lamare, and

Doc Rando. "Faz," as he was called, was an outstanding clarinetist; his ballads were exquisite, and his jazz work with the Bob Cats was top notch. His warm and beautiful tone is preserved on our recordings of "Sympathy" and "My Inspiration."

Faz's real name was Prestopnik, but when he was in Louis Prima's band, Louis could never pronounce it properly. He substituted, "Fa-Sol-La," from the childhood "Do-Rei-Mi" sequence, and it was "Fazola" from then on. He was a big eater and drinker, and weighed about 280 pounds. His typical breakfast was a dozen eggs and a few bottles of beer.

When we played the Earl Theater in Pittsburgh on New Year's Eve, he invited me for a drink before the midnight show. I ordered a scotch. He ordered the same—but asked for sixteen shots—and consumed them one by one!

During the show, when the Bob Cats were called to the front, "Faz" was the last to slowly climb down from the stand. When the spotlight hit him for his first solo, he was unable to move his fingers—the sound that emerged from his horn could have come from a steel pipe!

The band roared with laughter. Our trombonist Ray Conniff fell off the stand laughing so hard. That concluded our memorable New Year's Eve performance in Pittsburgh!

When Faz left the band in June 1940, he was briefly replaced by Hank D'Amico until Matty Matlock took over the clarinet chair.

Nappy Lamare, another founding member of the band, played rhythm guitar and banjo and handled the novelty vocals. He contributed several tunes to our repertoire including "Dixieland Shuffle" and "March of the Bob Cats." His real name was Hilton, and there are two versions of how he earned the "Nappy" nickname—his middle name was Napoleon, and he enjoyed frequent naps.

After World War II, Nappy, Ernani Bernardi, and Doc Rando opened "Club 47," a nightclub in Studio City named after Musicians Union Local 47. It employed only one musician, drummer Zutty Singleton, the rest of the nightly players were "sit-ins." Zutty also made the popular Creole Gumbo served at the club.

Yank Lawson was a wonderful trumpet player. He played great jazz with the Bob Cats. In the large band, he was the best section trumpet player I had ever worked with. His great feeling for the rhythm was encouraged by Ray Bauduc's propulsive two-beat drumming. Yank always waited for the last moment before standing up to play his fine solos, and he sat down immediately to resume with the section without missing a note.

After the Crosby band broke up, Yank and Bob Haggart continued their relationship as co-leaders of a popular recording group, the Lawson-Haggart Jazz Band, which eventually evolved into the World's Greatest Jazz Band. The WGJB sustained the swinging sounds that Lawson and Haggart conceived many years earlier with Crosby.

Matty Matlock was the arranger with the Bob Crosby band when I joined; he had been with them from the start. He did not play clarinet with us until after Irving Fazola left. Matty was an avid golfer, and always had his clubs with him wherever we appeared.

On one of our engagements in Catalina, while we were playing on the local course, he accidentally drove a ball that struck another golfer and caused a severe head injury. We tried to reach a doctor, but learned that Matty had injured the only M.D. on the island!

Eddie Miller, the great tenor sax player, had also been in the Crosby band since it began. He played in the full orchestra and with the Bob Cats, and often ranked "Number One" by *Down Beat* and *Metronome* magazines. Eddie, at that time, was one of very few saxophonists whose sound and style fit into a Dixieland setting. He had the best "ear" of any musician I ever had the pleasure of working with. Eddie could fake more songs without seeing the music than anybody I ever knew—and keys made no difference. If he had not played a tune before, he would say to me, "Max, what note does it start on?"—and away he went with that beautiful sound!

Buddy Morrow (Moe Zudacoff), from New Haven, Connecticut, became a popular freelance studio trombonist in New York City while still in his teens. Buddy, whose nickname was "Muni," led Crosby's great trombone section alongside Elmer Smithers and Floyd O'Brien during the band's last year. Before joining Crosby, he held the lead trombone chair in bands led by Artie Shaw, Bunny Berigan, Eddie Duchin, Paul Whiteman, and Tommy Dorsey. Since Dorsey's death, Buddy has led the orchestra for the last 24 years.

Arthur "Doc" Rando was an excellent saxophonist and clarinetist. He was recommended by Irving Fazola and Ray Bauduc and joined the band about six months after I became a member. "Doc" was not a nickname. He was an experienced M.D., but abandoned his busy medical practice in New Orleans during the Depression because patients were unable to pay for his services. He was a master diagnostician and always gave us the best advice possible or referred us to many of his medical colleagues around the country. "Doc" is now retired in Las Vegas, but still helps musicians in need of medical attention.

Gil Rodin was a member of the Ben Pollack Orchestra when it broke up in 1934. The following year, he organized a new band with Pollack's sidemen and recorded under the pseudonym Clark Randall and His Orchestra. When Bob Crosby assumed leadership, Gil continued playing clarinet and saxophone, and assumed the roles of music director and band manager. His musicianship and business acumen contributed greatly to the band's success.

He was a fine section player, but not a very good soloist, and seldom was given a featured spot. During 1940, *Down Beat* magazine was publishing transcribed solos by famous jazz artists. As a joke, the band arranged for the magazine to print a "special blues solo by Gil Rodin." The first twelve bars were one sustained note!

He wrote "Boogie Woogie Maxixe" which was popularized by Crosby's recording in 1939. He later became a valued executive at Universal Studios and MCA Records in Los Angeles, and left the firm to complete his autobiography, "The Swinging Years—I Was There."

In 1940, he was honored by *Down Beat* magazine as an "Immortal of Jazz." Gil studied the art and technology of television and soon became the producer of Bob Crosby's TV show. He also produced the Jack Benny Show and two jazz documentaries, "The Swinging Years" and "The Singing Swinging Years."

Warren Smith was in the band when I joined. "Smitty" was a true "tailgate" trombonist as heard in the Bob Cat's recordings, especially on "Till We Meet Again," a number they recorded a few days before I joined the band. The record was so popular, the Bob Cats had to play it almost every night.

When "Smitty" left us in 1940, he was replaced by Floyd O'Brien, a fine Chicago trombonist, who had recently held a trombone chair in Gene Krupa's band. Like "Smitty," Floyd was a masterful slide artist and fit well in our Dixieland format for the big band and the Bob Cats.

During the post-war years, "Smitty" appeared with Lu Watters' Yerba Buena Jazz Band at "Hambone Kelly's" in El Cerrito, California, and recorded several tunes with them. He re-joined Bob Crosby briefly before launching a successful free-lance career on the West Coast.

Muggsy Spanier, the noted Chicago cornetist, joined the band on June 1, 1940 after sitting-in with us at the Blackhawk in Chicago.

There was one major problem. We played intricate arrangements written by Bob Haggart, Matty Matlock, Paul Weston, and Ray Conniff—but Muggsy, who was a great jazzman, and played wonderfully by ear, did not read music! He was featured in the full orchestra playing third trumpet and handled all the hot choruses which he improvised beautifully.

During our weekly NBC radio show, the band played eight numbers. Bob paid me $20.00 extra to teach Muggsy the arrangements before each broadcast. It was amazing how well he remembered the arrangements after he learned them. Muggsy also played with the Bob Cats, our band within the band, which always had a feature spot on broadcasts, but these were improvised, and he handled the Dixieland tunes masterfully.

I made only one recording with the Bob Cats. It was in December 1940. The full Crosby band accompanied Bing Crosby on "San Antonio Rose" and "It Makes No Difference

Now" (Decca 3590). Muggsy was there, but since we had no advance information about Bing's scheduled tunes, I was unable to coach him about the arrangements, so I played the trumpet parts that included a short melodic solo on "San Antonio Rose."

During "It Makes No Difference Now," there was a Dixieland interlude in the arrangement for the Bob Cats, and I played with them, since there was no time to teach Muggsy the tune.

Jess Stacy and I, as mentioned earlier, joined the Crosby band on the same day. On our second record date, we recorded Bob Haggart's arrangement of Jess' "Complainin'," which, until the band broke-up during the war, became another one of our most requested numbers.

Jess practiced constantly. He carried a silent keyboard on our band bus and practiced throughout our journeys. In a *Metronome* magazine interview some months after he joined the band, Bob Crosby said, "The band is playing cleaner, the arrangements sound better, and the enthusiasm is greater. Jess Stacy put us in the right groove!"

Although Jess was probably Benny Goodman's favorite pianist, he preferred playing with us because there was less tension. Goodman was a perfectionist, especially on intonation. Jess told us, "Between each set, Benny had me pounding an A on the piano so the reeds and brass could remain in perfect tune. After Bob Crosby hired me, I continued my habit of hitting the A key between sets. Until, one night when Bob said to me, 'If you strike that damn key once more, I'll give you your five years' notice!' "

Paul Weston, (Paul Wetstein, Jr.) who did some arranging for us, had previously written for Tommy Dorsey. In the '20s, he played string bass and tuba with several bands, including Hal Kemp. Paul formed his own orchestra when he left Crosby in 1940, and gained fame as conductor and arranger for his wife, Jo Stafford. Together, they helped launch the recently formed Capitol Records.

Zeke Zarchy ranks highly among the first trumpeters of the world. He recommended me as his replacement when he left Crosby to join Tommy Dorsey's orchestra. Coincidentally, Zeke was also my predecessor in the Joe Haymes band three years earlier. I always admired his playing, and his shoes were hard to fill.

Chapter Four
Romance on the High Cs

During a one-week engagement in 1939 with the Eddie DeLange band in Cedar Point, near Cleveland, Ohio, I met Ida Steinberg who was on vacation with some of her girl-friends. Although I only knew Ida for a few days, I was impressed with everything about her. Unfortunately, I was unable to court her because I was on the road all the time—but I never forgot her.

After we exchanged a few letters, and had several phone conversations, I felt it was unfair for her to have any expectations about our relationship.

I had not reached my goal to be a trumpet player in the Bob Crosby band, and I was not in a financial position to make a commitment.

A year later, when I had achieved that prized objective, the Crosby band was booked in Cedar Point, where I met Ida earlier. I wrote to her and expressed a desire to see her again, but she did not reply. When I called from Cedar Point, Ida told me that her mother would not allow her to come there. I asked her to bring her mother. When she did not come, I borrowed a car from our trombonist Ray Conniff and drove to Cleveland after work one night to visit Ida; I had not seen her for a year.

It was about 4:00 A.M. when I arrived, and we talked until 7:00 A.M. when her mother awoke and made our breakfast. I drove Ida to work and returned to Cedar Point to play the job that night. From then on, I called her every week.

In January 1941, the Crosby band was scheduled to play a three-month engagement at the Mark Hopkins Hotel in San Francisco followed by a Chicago booking at the Sherman Hotel's famed Panther Room. I called Ida's mother from San Francisco and told her I would like to know her daughter better, and invited them both to come to Chicago. This time she allowed her daughter to come—alone. I assured her that Ida would have her own room, and there would be no problems. She trusted me, and Ida arrived on Sunday.

It was the band's day off, and we had an exciting time together. The first day Ida was there, I asked her to marry me, and she agreed! She called her mother with the news and asked her to come to Chicago to discuss the wedding.

The three of us saw the sights, visited the clubs, and talked about our marriage plans. I suggested that it take place in my hometown, since I had a very large family in Rhode Island, and had been away for so long. Ida agreed. She and her mother went to Providence and spent a month with my family preparing for the large wedding.

Bob Crosby agreed to let me off for that week, and I arranged for Abe Dworkin, a fine trumpet player, to take my place during the band's theater engagement in Columbus, Ohio. (I mentioned earlier that I met Abe years before while I was playing a Columbus hotel job with Clint Noble's orchestra.)

After I played Crosby's five Friday shows with Abe Dworkin seated at my side, I left for Providence. I arrived on Saturday morning, and went directly to the North Providence Town Hall to obtain our marriage license. The building was closed on Saturday, but my father was a well-known city pioneer, and a good friend of Louis Sweet, the town clerk. He opened the building, and while he and my father had a drink together, he prepared my license.

Our elaborate wedding took place on May 11, 1941. Since I was the hometown boy that reached a high level in my profession, there was a parade for me from the "four corners" in North Providence to my family's farmhouse, led by the mayor and supervised by the chief of police.

Ida and I left the following day for Buffalo to rejoin the band. We were working our way to California, and Crosby arranged for us to purchase new cars the next week in Detroit. Bob and Gil Rodin bought Cadillacs, Yank Lawson bought a Chrysler. My choice was a new Buick, and the rest of the band bought various cars—from one broker/dealer.

We continued on the road in caravan style, playing theaters, one-nighters, and college proms on the way to California for a six-week booking at the Catalina Island Casino Ballroom—and our eventual honeymoon!

Then we settled in Hollywood where the Bob Crosby band played in several films, including *Sis Hopkins* with Judy Canova in 1941 and *Holiday Inn* with Fred Astaire and Bing Crosby in 1942.

During this pleasant period in California, I renewed my friendship with several musicians I met while we were traveling around the country. I knew most of them during my big band experience in the East, but now, many were in the radio, TV, and motion picture studio orchestras in which I played for many years.

Chapter Five
The War Years

By 1942, we were involved in World War II, and my draft classification as 1-A was still registered in North Providence, RI. The governor of Rhode Island called to personally tell me that my number was coming up shortly and said that many service bands were formed there and I would be welcomed by many of them. Ida was pregnant then, and we did not want to go back to the cold weather.

Fortunately, a Coast Guard band of professional musicians was being assembled, and, in October, an officer visited the Bob Crosby band while we were playing at the Rendezvous Ballroom in Balboa, California. He was looking for recruits. I immediately volunteered.

This was on Saturday night. On the following Monday, I enlisted as a First Class Petty Officer. My assignment was to play first trumpet in the 11th Naval Coast Guard Band that was formed in Wilmington, California under the direction of Rudy Vallee. The famed West Coast bandleader Jimmy Grier was our assistant leader.

This all-star band included members of the country's most prominent orchestras. Among them were: Andy Secrest, trumpet (Paul Whiteman); Dave Wade, trumpet (Raymond Scott Quintet); Bert Harry, trumpet (Ray Noble); King Jackson, trombone (Spike Jones); and saxophonists Sam Rubinwich and Mickey Folus (Woody Herman). Our group also included Redd Harper, a country-western composer and trumpet player who was a member of Jimmy Grier's civilian band. He was a great entertainer and a big hit in all our performances.

When we practiced our marching drills at the Coast Guard base, our leader Rudy Vallee usually was not present, so he was not familiar with the drum major signals. On one marching review he decided to handle the baton. He gave us the wrong signal—he went his way, and the band marched directly toward a brick wall! After that, he allowed the drum major to give the signals. Rudy Vallee, a famous star in civilian life, was not a great musician or singer, but he was a fine M.C. and knew how to put on a good show. He could talk to the audience for hours, hold their attention, and receive tremendous ovations. Bob Crosby had similar skills. Both leaders appreciated their musicians and always introduced us with kind words.

Rudy was very proud of our band, and we were soon traveling all over the U.S. entertaining servicemen and women in Army, Navy, Air Force, and Marine bases. We also played for war bond drives, and made recordings for distribution to the services.

We traveled in all types of planes. Once, in a flying fortress, I crawled into the gunner's nose bubble to watch our landing at a remote Iowa base. We over-ran the short runway and finally stopped in a farmer's field. No one was injured, and the plane was not damaged; but I was terrified seeing the ground appear so suddenly and watching the corn stalks flying around us! That was the last time I ever entered the nose cone!

During our war bond performance in a packed New York auditorium, the service office in charge was an arrogant army major. He tried to tell Rudy how to run his show. That was a big mistake—nobody ever told him how to run a show! An argument followed, and Rudy told the major, "Go f—- yourself!"

Since the major out-ranked him, this was insubordination—a very serious charge in the armed services. The military authorities were advised and a special hearing took place in Washington, D.C. We all expected a severe reprimand and, possibly, a court martial.

When they learned that our New York show broke all previous sales records for war bonds, the bossy major was relieved of his position, and they elevated Rudy's rank! That's what I call military justice!

In March of 1945, our Coast Guard band was assigned to a troop ship, the *Admiral Eberle*, and we sailed for the South Pacific with fifty-five hundred soldiers and marines. Rudy Vallee retired and Lieutenant Junior Grade Jimmy Grier became our leader. Later, Elliot Daniel took over the band as assistant leader.

Our band entertained service personnel aboard many Navy ships and in several camps and hospitals in New Guinea, the Philippines, and other islands. One Sunday, at Manos in the Admiralty Islands, we were playing a concert aboard our ship, when a Navy plane, making friendly dives toward us, crashed on the deck and the pilot was killed. He was a war hero who shot down twenty-two Japanese planes and was due to go home soon. Amid much confusion on the deck, the musicians were first to reach our many injured crewmen, and they administered assistance until medics arrived.

Later, we encountered a horrible typhoon. Servicemen were extremely ill throughout the ship, and the medical staff was overwhelmed. Many musicians in the ship's company volunteered to assist the doctors wherever possible.

We were in the first convoy of 100 ships that landed in Manila. Our ship had the assignment to take about 300

American civilians previously held in Japanese prison camps back to the United States. Based on the achievements of our band, Captain Towle, our ship's head officer, was elevated to the rank of Admiral.

When the war ended, our troop ship returned to its home port in Wilmington, California. Although we were to be released from service in a few days, our band was scheduled to lead a parade in Arizona. Our audience was in a reviewing stand, filled with top Coast Guard officers and city officials.

The fifty musicians had already begun celebrating their forthcoming release, and the band's marching formation was bizarre. The drum major gave us the wrong marching signals and had difficulty walking in a straight line. One of our trumpet players staggered out of the formation to chat with some young girls watching the parade. Some musicians, too drunk to play, just held their horns as we passed the reviewing stand. I am sure we sounded awful!

After the parade, we were to play a concert in a huge auditorium. Our leader, Jimmy Grier, a very talented composer and conductor, also had been "celebrating" our last days in the Coast Guard. We were all seated in position when Jimmy staggered onto the stage, bowed to the large audience, mounted the podium, and gave us the downbeat to start the concert.

He swung his baton with gusto—too much gusto. He fell sprawling among the first row of musicians! With the nonchalance of a pro, he slowly rose, dusted himself off, and continued the concert. We feared that this embarrassment, coupled with our poor parade performance, would provoke the Coast Guard Brass to throw us all in the "brig" instead of discharging us from the service.

Fortunately, everything worked out O.K. We played a

good concert, and our ship's captain, resplendent in his new admiral's uniform, warmly congratulated each of us. We returned to California and re-entered civilian life.

Chapter Six
The Post-War Hollywood Scene

When I was in the Coast Guard, they provided Ida with naval housing in Long Beach, California, not far from our base. Our daughter Marlene and son Barry were born there.

I was released from the Coast Guard in November 1945, and we purchased a small house in North Hollywood. I joined Musicians Union Local 47 and began playing briefly with some local big bands in theaters, and on radio and TV shows, but I continued looking for steady work.

During that period, I played first trumpet in bands led by Jan Savitt, George Kates, Jimmy Grier, Anson Weeks, Mickey Katz, Claude Gordon, Lud Gluskin, Al Newman, Bill Hatch, and Victor Young.

One day, in front of NBC on Vine Street, I ran into the trumpet star Mannie Klein who was a fan of the Bob Crosby band, and often heard me play with the band. I told him I was not going on the road again and would appreciate his help.

Mannie's brother Dave Klein, also a fine trumpeter (featured in the Ted Lewis band earlier), was the number one contractor for radio at NBC, CBS, and ABC.

Mannie told him, "Max Herman plays first trumpet as good as anybody you have, so please help him!"

A day later I got a call from Dave Klein to report to CBS

on Sunday and play trumpet on the *Beulah* show, I walked into the studio and met the leader Al Sachs and the contractor Ward Archer. They asked me to play third trumpet. I wanted to work and said, "Yes!"

The "Beulah" show's theme had a very high trumpet part, and since I weighed only 120 pounds and was very thin, they thought I could not handle those high notes, despite Mannie and Dave Klein's recommendation.

Our rehearsal started with the theme, and one of the other two trumpet players tried to play it. He didn't come close. Then the leader asked the other trumpet player to try. He also failed. It was very near showtime and the leader had no choice, so he suggested I attempt it. I played it with ease, and from then, my reputation in Hollywood spread fast.

I received a call to play for conductor Wilbur Hatch on a major radio show. Mannie Klein was also in the orchestra. When he arrived, I was seated in the second chair. Mannie said, "Move over to the first chair, Max. Wilbur knows how I play, but I want him to hear you." I played many shows for Wilbur after that.

Soon, I had seven jobs on radio and TV. I was fortunate to play on major network shows with Ed Wynn, Burns and Allen, and many other radio and TV stars—thanks to Mannie Klein's generous assistance. (He was always very helpful to musicians. I will tell you more about Mannie later.)

Musicians in the studio orchestras had to be excellent "readers." Perhaps we would have an initial "run through," but after that, we were expected to play the music perfectly. When vocalists requested a "special" key for their number, we also were expected to transpose on sight. Thanks to my early training with Alexander Billincoff, I had no problem with those tasks.

During this period, I played many engagements with society bandleader, Mannie Harmon, who was very popular with the Hollywood film colony. Ronald Reagan selected him to play at the 1956 Republican Convention. Mannie held that role until 1992! When asked if he was a Republican, he always replied, "I only belong to the 'Cocktail Party!' "

After a few busy seasons in Hollywood, Ida and I decided I should take the summer off and bring Marlene and Barry to North Providence, Rhode Island, to spend several weeks on the farm with my parents.

I happened to run into clarinetist Gus Bivona, my colleague in the Hudson-DeLange band before the war. He had recently left Benny Goodman. His wife, singer Ruth Robin, who Gus met when they were both in the Jan Savitt orchestra, was very ill. They were staying in a hotel and needed a place to live. Since our North Hollywood home would be empty for six or seven weeks, Ida and I offered our home to Gus and his wife.

Before we left for Providence, Gus asked me if Buddy DeFranco and his wife could live with them since Gus' wife needed help. We agreed, and the four of them stayed for the summer. When it approached the time for us to come home, Buddy decided to do some yard work before we returned. He is a great clarinetist, winner of many jazz awards, but he knew little about gardening. He diligently removed everything across the front of our house—including Ida's prize rose bushes!

We still jokingly admonish Buddy about his futile horticultural efforts.

Baseball as a Pastime

Since 1908, when Albert Von Tilzer wrote his famed "Take Me Out to the Ball Game," the tune has been the national anthem of "America's Pastime." My interest in the game dates from my grammar school days in Woodville, the small farm village in North Providence, Rhode Island, where I later managed the local Woodville Townies.

Many big name orchestras had ball teams and traveled with a full set of baseball equipment and team uniforms. When the bands were on the road, they played hotly contested afternoon games with other bands, or college bands—even penitentiary bands!

Harry James was the captain and starting pitcher in Benny Goodman's team. When James formed his own band, Buddy Rich was the center fielder. Frank Sinatra played right field, but his batting average was only about .200. The current joke at that time involved the bandleader's interrogation of prospect band members. Batting averages were as important as their musical skills!

During the postwar years, many actors, writers, musicians, agents, and publishers settled in Southern California. Since the weather was moderate all year, many of us congregated at parks in Los Angeles, Hollywood, and Beverly Hills to play softball.

Composers Sammy Cahn and Julie Styne furnished most of the equipment and they acted as managers and picked the sides. The game became very popular and several regular teams were organized. Film stars like Phil Silvers and Tony Curtis also participated. At times, Dinah Shore and Carmen Miranda sponsored teams and supplied equipment and uniforms.

Dinah's team was very good. The roster included outstanding musicians like George Wald, Ted and Dick Nash,

Dave Pell, and Jimmy Clark. I played in the outfield with my brothers Nate and Joe. I was a fair ball player, but not in their class. I am sure that if they were teenagers today, Nate and Joe would both be potential million-dollar major-league prospects.

We were invited to join a league with teams from NBC, CBS, ABC, Capitol Records, and radio station KFWB. We won so many games that the other teams issued an ultimatum—Nate and Joe Herman and George Wald could no longer play on the same team, or the other league members would not compete with us!

I take pride in having successfully managed Little League teams and teams in the Babe Ruth and American Legion Leagues. The kids' parents became involved and expected their children to bat like big leaguers. I taught all my team members to have confidence in themselves. As a result, they became good hitters. We won more games than we lost, and everyone had a good time.

My daughter Marlene, who is now a successful attorney, was always a great baseball fan and she reminded me of a situation that occurred in one of my Little League games. A widowed mother came to me with her plump young son who had no baseball talents but wanted to be on my team. It was near the end of the season, but I never turned anyone away.

In the final game of the year, the score was tied, and we had three men on base. It was the last of the ninth inning and we had two outs. It was a high-scoring game, and everyone on the roster had been at bat—except my recent recruit, the plump child whose mother was in the audience. I put him in as a pinch hitter.

The opposing pitcher was throwing some wild balls, so I told the boy to stand very close to the plate, and not to swing at any ball. He followed my instructions, and the pitcher walked him. The youngster, responsible for the winning run that walked home, was the hero of the game. He probably has never forgotten the incident—neither have I!

Some of my American Legion players showed great potential for the big leagues. I wanted them to go to college, where I had good contacts with the college coaches, but the big-league signing bonuses looked good to the boys and their parents. A few were signed, but never became stars.

I had two outstanding seventeen-year-old pitchers who won many games for me. I could get college athletic scholarships for them, and promises from major-league scouts that they would watch their progress in collegiate competition. Both boys soon signed major-league contracts. Unfortunately, instead of giving them a chance to develop properly, eager minor-league managers pressed them to throw as hard as possible. Their potentially great pitching arms were ruined by following that advice.

My son Barry became a second-generation ball player. He inherited his considerable skills from his uncles, Nate and Joe—not from me. In a Babe Ruth League game, Barry hit three successive home runs. He was intentionally walked during his subsequent times at bat!

Throughout the years, I enjoyed many experiences as a baseball player, coach, and manager. When the Musician's Union team played the Hollywood Stars at Dodger Stadium, Jimmie Clark, a business agent, was on our team. He was a terrific ballplayer and could excel on any of the nine positions.

I played center field for the Union, and I managed to catch a fly ball—although I was well into my fifties. I hit a single my first time at bat. The next time, I hit the ball over the center fielder's head—it looked like a sure triple!

I struggled running to first base. My fifty-year-old legs

told me that was as far as I could go. Our first base coach, Union President, John Tranchitella, said, "Max, congratulations! You are the only player I have seen who could stretch a triple into a single!"

The Publishing Business

As a staff studio trumpet player for many years, I always felt that the composers on radio and TV did not receive proper credit for their music. They were paid an initial fee for their work, but the networks assumed all publishing rights. The composers received no compensation for additional performances, and the networks collected the ASCAP royalties on all the material.

I formed Herman Music, an ASCAP publishing company in 1952, and asked the bandleaders to give me the publishing rights to their music. Many agreed, and soon Herman Music controlled the material from *Gunsmoke, Laurel and Hardy, The Whistler* and many others.

CBS attorneys opposed my actions, but my attorney quickly threatened them with an anti-trust suit and I retained the publishing rights. As a result, the composers I represented still receive performance royalties from ASCAP whenever their compositions are used, and earn fees from recordings made of their material.

I was also able to obtain publishing rights for songs in Billy Graham's religious films through my Coast Guard colleague, Redd Harper, who starred in those movies. His big hit, "Each Step of the Way," came from one of those pictures. Redd and I formed the BMI publishing firm Fiesta Music for this material and sold thousands of sheet music copies with Redd's picture on the cover.

Fiesta Music's reputation spread and our catalog soon

listed over six hundred religious songs including some written by Dale Evans (Mrs. Roy Rogers), Ralph Carmichael, and Dr. Oswald Smith. Jo Stafford, with her conductor-husband Paul Weston, an ex-Bob Crosby bandmember, recorded songs from both of my publishing firms. The famed blues singer, Jimmy Witherspoon, also recorded several songs from the two catalogs.

As a publisher of religious and secular songs, we dealt with several talented composers. They all trusted us with their music, and appreciated the care we took to see that they received proper royalties. We have all remained friends through the years.

To this day, after more than half a century, the *Gunsmoke* TV theme, of which I still own the publishing rights, is still contributing to my way of life.

Chapter Seven

The Complete Change of the A.F. of M. and Its New Policies

In 1946 and 1947, during the transition from radio to television, our musicians experienced a severe depression because of policies instituted by American Federation of Musicians President Jimmy Petrillo.

Many major radio shows like the *Jack Benny Show,* and *Gunsmoke,* had musicians' contracts that provided residuals on all re-runs to leaders, sidemen, arrangers, etc. Petrillo arbitrarily changed the contracts so all residual monies would go into the A.F. of M. Trust Fund. He also assessed TV producers with a fee of 5 percent of their total production costs payable to the Trust Fund.

The broadcast industry would not accept these staunch conditions, and arranged for program music to be recorded by foreign orchestras. As a result, we studio musicians were all out of work.

Marty Berman was responsible for involving me in Union politics. We worked together in the Eddie DeLange band. He was aware of my earlier political activity in Rhode Island and asked me to be the political strategist and I joined the leaders of the revolt against Petrillo's actions.

Meetings, held in our home in North Hollywood, were attended by prominent musicians and bandleaders interested in opposing the unpopular Federation's edicts. Our first move, to attain an official voice in our action, was to elect one of us to a Local 47 office. There was an opening for vice president on the next ballot, and we chose Cecil Read to run against the incumbent. He won by a large majority. We were also able to elect a few from our group to the Local 47 Board of Directors.

Unfortunately, Jimmy Petrillo denied all our requests to modify his demands on radio and TV producers. The programs were still using imported music, and our studio musicians were still out of work. To address the problem, we arranged a general meeting attended by over three thousand musicians at the Hollywood Palladium in 1954.

Supreme Court Justice Arthur Goldberg was then head consul for the Steel Workers Union. He held open hearings for five days at the request of Jimmy Petrillo. Goldberg heard charges against Cecil Read and thirteen musicians who spoke during the Local 47 General Meeting and at a private meeting.

Justice Goldberg ruled that the meetings were a violation of American Federation of Musicians' by-laws and recommended a five-year expulsion for Cecil Read for infringement of the by-laws, and one year each for the thirteen other members who spoke at the private meeting that was illegally taped.

To this day, I think this was a bad decision since the meeting was to plan action and lawsuits against the American Federation of Musicians.

Cecil Read and union members suggested a campaign to raise funds for legal advice regarding instituting the suit against the A.F. of M. and the Trust Fund. At a *Gunsmoke* rehearsal for a live radio broadcast, starring William Conrad as Matt Dillon, U.S. Marshall, Dale Brown and I were in the orchestra. Dale played clarinet and trombone and I was the only trumpet player. We launched the "Musicians Defense Fund" that day with the plan to collect one dollar from musicians as they participated in recordings for films, TV, phonograph records, radio, and commercials.

Envelopes were placed on music stands at every session for their dollar contribution. Bandleaders and contractors contributed more. Frank Sinatra placed a 100-dollar bill in an envelope every week during his broadcast rehearsals.

The captains in each studio collected the envelopes and gave them to a committee headed by Uan Rasey. Eventually we raised $260,000.

While we were working on the lawsuits, Cecil Read, who did not feel we were getting anywhere with Jimmy Petrillo, formed his own Guild. Some Los Angeles musicians voted for the Guild to represent them in dealings with motion picture and TV producers and local record companies.

I can honestly say that I experienced the worst period of my musical life. Dissension over these issues between Cecil Read's Guild and the Union disrupted friendships of long standing; even families were involved. Although our aims were identical, we all wanted more work for musicians, but bitter lawsuits were considered.

Many of us who did not join the Guild felt we could then change the Federation's position since Jimmy Petrillo had resigned and Herman Kenin, the new A.F. of M. President, promised to moderate Petrillo's unreasonable demands on the broadcast industry.

During this period, we elected a whole slate of officers with Elliot Daniel as president, John Tranchitella as vice-president—and I was secretary. The new Local 47 President, Elliot Daniel, who served with me in the Coast Guard, was an accomplished composer. His credits in-

49

cluded the *I Love Lucy* theme, *Lavender Hill,* etc. He wanted to serve only one term, so, in 1958, Tranchitella advanced to the presidency, and I became vice-president.

We were successful with our lawsuit and obtained a settlement of seven million dollars for legal expenses and payments to musicians. The *Jack Benny Show* bandmembers each received over $10,000. The *Gunsmoke* players received $3,500, and musicians on other programs were awarded varying amounts.

Herman Kenin, aware that the two organizations could not be the solution, met with Cecil Read and persuaded him to dissolve the Guild. There was no further action against the musicians, and Guild members resumed their union affiliation with no record of them ever leaving.

We were one solidified union again—thanks to the pressure extended by the Guild, the Supreme Court ruling, President Kenin's guidance, and the resolve of all the musicians. Unfortunately, until this was finally settled, many members lost an entire year of employment in the studios.

As a result of the bitter dispute, we arranged for part of the Congressional Labor Committee, Phil Landrum, Joe Holt, and Jimmy Roosevelt to come to Hollywood for hearings regarding our complaints. As an aftermath of the hearings, Congress adapted the Landrum-Griffin Act in the mid '50s. Along with the Taft-Hartley Laws, it mandated important conditions that were not favorable to labor.

Perry Borrelli and his orchestra—Providence, Rhode Island—1927; Max Herman, age 13, second from left

Joe Haymes—1937

Eddie DeLange and his orchestra—Elitch Gardens, Denver, Colorado—1937; Max Herman, top row, second from right

From Gus Arnheim's band, Memphis, Tennessee—1937: Max Herman, Lou Singer, Stan Kenton, Dave Frankel

Max Herman with his parents, Rose and Sam Herman—1937

The Will Hudson Orchestra's jazz combo, New York—1938: Doc Goldberg—bass, Max Herman—watching, Buss Etri—guitar, Mark Hyams—piano, Joe Bauer—trumpet, Billy Exner—drums, Gus Bivona—clarinet, (unknown—saxophone), Jack Andrews—trombone, Gigi Bohn—saxophone.

The Bob Crosby trumpet section, 1940: Muggsy Spanier, Max Herman, Al King

The Bob Crosby Orchestra, Chicago, 1940; bottom row, left to right: Max Herman, Eddie Miller, Doris Day, Bob Crosby, Warren Smith; middle row, left to right: Jess Stacy, "Doc" Rando, Irving Fazola, Billy Butterfield, Gil Rodin; top row, left to right: George Koenig, Ray Bauduc, Nappy Lamare, Ray Conniff, Bob Haggart, Bob Peck

Down Beat magazine ad—June 1, 1940

Ida and Max Herman on their wedding day—May 11, 1941

Brass section of the Bob Crosby Orchestra—1941; during recording for the Bing Crosby/Fred Astaire Paramount film *Holiday Inn*; front row, left to right: Floyd O'Brien, Buddy Morrow, Elmer Smith; back row, left to right: Frank Zinzer, Lyman Vunk, Max Herman, Bob Crosby, Mannie Klein

The Bob Crosby Orchestra—Casino ballroom, Catalina Island—1942; bottom row, left to right: Nappy Lamare, Eddie Miller, Artie Mendelson, Max Herman, "Doc" Rando, Floyd O'Brien, Matty Matlock, Gil Rodin; top row, left to right: Jess Stacy, Ray Bauduc, Elmer Smithers, Yank Lawson, Bob Crosby, Liz Tilton, Bob Haggart, Lyman Vunk, Buddy Morrow, Tony Paris

Trumpet section of the Coast Guard band—Hollywood Canteen—1944; left to right: Redd Harper, Al Ruby, Max Herman, Bert Harry, Andy Secrest, Eddie Ramos, Dave Wade

Hollywood Bowl—1970: Robert Wagner, Max Herman, Ernest Fleischman, Jay Rubinoff

Three trumpet giants—1975: Teddy Buckner, Max Herman, and Mannie Klein

Max Herman and Zubin Mehta—1976

Ida and Max Herman, greeted by His Royal Highness Brumibol Adulyadej, King of Thailand—1993

The Herman brothers: Joe, Nate, and Max

Chapter Eight
Union Politics

I am often asked "Why did you accept a full-time job as a union official and give up playing music?" I felt the need of a more stable position. Ida and I were building a new big house. Our daughter, Marlene, was attending U.C.L.A., and our son, Barry, was about to enter dental school at U.S.C.

Being a union officer did not affect my successful publishing business which earned more than I could make as a professional trumpet player. And, I sincerely wanted to help the union provide a better service to its members.

When I became president of Local 47 in Hollywood in 1972, I sold my Fiesta Publishing firm to the Zondervam Bible Company but retained my secular publishing company. As Union president, the first man I hired as my assistant was Cecil Read. I think his greatest accomplishment was obtaining ratification rights on all contracts for musicians in their respective fields.

I served as president of Local 47 from 1972 to 1983 and from 1990 to 1993 and never lost an election. In addition, I also served during five two-year terms on the International Board of the American Federation of Musicians.

As union president, I was always proud of my relationship with the Police Department, the City Council, the County Board of Supervisors, and State Officials. The Los Angeles Police Department had a wonderful labor detail with whom I worked very closely. Whenever it became necessary to picket non-union venues, there were never serious problems—thanks to the professional manner in which the L.A.P.D. coordinated our rights with the rights of the firms involved.

I always felt I had the best-qualified members on my Board of Directors and Trial Boards, and considered myself only the manager of a very good team. I was always proud of selecting my Board of Directors that were experts in many fields and could properly represent union members. That is why we became an outstandingly successful union. I look back, with pride, on some of our memorable achievements.

Together, we helped create the great Musicians' Pension Fund of which I became the trustee. We arranged to have a professional auditor/accountant in-house who made weekly financial reports to the Board of Directors, and I never commented to the press without having a professional public relations expert at my side.

I spoke to most of my union executive colleagues every day, and they all made reports during our weekly board meetings. I want to mention just a few who added their wisdom and knowledge that helped me chart the direction of Local 47 during the years I was president:

Benny Carter, one of the principal architects of the golden era of big bands; **Buddy Collette,** great jazz woodwind player and composer; **Irving Bush,** prominent trumpet player with the Los Angeles Symphony Orchestra; **Eddie Cano,** Latin pianist and recording artist; **Abe Most,** jazz clarinetist selected by record firms to re-create the sounds of Benny Goodman, Artie Shaw, Barney Bigard, etc.; **Marl Young,** conductor-composer of the music on Lucille Ball's TV series; **Nellie Lutcher,** great jazz pianist, vocalist, and entertainer. She advised me on the twelve hundred night clubs, restaurants, ballrooms, and hotels that hired Local 47 musicians; **Ray Siegel,** principal bassist with the Chicago Symphony Orchestra and the Los Angeles Philharmonic; **Russ Freeman,** world-renowned jazz pianist; **Bill Hughes,** popular music executive and contractor, **Catherine Gotthoffer,** excellent harpist in the film and TV studios; **Spud Murphy,** composer, arranger, bandleader, and teacher; and **Jay Cooper,** attorney for the stars.

I also engaged labor lawyer **Bob Rissman,** CPA **Ralph Holmes,** public relations consulars and writers, **Leonard Shane** and **Jerry Lench,**—plus my wife of sixty-four years, **Ida Herman,** who expertly edited everything I wrote. She and our good friend, **Dr. Frances Berres,** were the final editors of all the literature that went to our union members before every election.

As president of Local 47, I felt that each member was my friend. I reprsented them all regardless of their roles in the music business, or the styles of music they played—Latin, Country-Western, Big Bands, Symphonies, Opera, Studios, etc.

During my years in office, many problems and disputes were amicably settled in informal meetings with the principals involved. Here are some of the memorable incidents that occurred during my presidency:

The New Orleans clarinetist, Pete Fountain, has been a legend for many years. In 1959, his fame spread when he was a featured TV artist on the weekly "Lawrence Welk Show."

After a few years with Welk, Pete came to my office and asked me to help him resolve a dilemma. He wanted to return to New Orleans to play with his small band, but his contract with Welk did not expire for two more years. He did not know how to handle the situation.

I had a very good relationship with Welk and his manager Sam Lutz. I invited them and Pete to my office and told Lawrence that Pete appreciated the importance of his weekly TV appearances with his band, but he was a homesick boy, and wanted to return to New Orleans. Lawrence promptly agreed to tear up Pete's contract.

During the peak of Elvis Presley's fame, he was scheduled to appear in Los Angeles at a major concert. He planned to use a large local orchestra with his small traveling group. On the day of the sold-out concert, Local 47 had not received the contract to cover the services of our musicians. A contract was mandatory before the concert could begin, so I called Elvis' manager, Colonel Tom Parker, whom I knew personally.

He apologized for the oversight, and promised that the document would be on my desk the next day. With only this verbal "handshake," we allowed the musicians to play that evening. When I arrived at the office the next day, the contract was there!

That afternoon, I had a surprise visitor. My office door opened, and Elvis Presley, standing with his hand against the door frame, said, "Mr. Herman, I want to thank you for helping to make my concert such a great success," and left.

When I told my teenage daughter Marlene about the event, she and her girlfriends, all dedicated Elvis Presley fans, came the next day—and kissed the spot on the door frame where his hand had been pressed!

Pat Brown was a great California governor who could communicate with people in every walk of life. We became very good friends. In 1966, when he was campaigning for re-election against Ronald Reagan, there was a big rally for him. Louis Armstrong was a special guest, and Governor Brown asked me to join him to escort Louis to the podium.

Louis said to me, "Max, I heard the Crosby band frequently and I wish I could play first trumpet like you." I have never forgotten those fine words from the great man.

California has not had a governor of Pat Brown's stature since then. He would have made a great Supreme Court Justice.

Chapter Nine
"Bringing Broadway to Hollywood"

Hollywood was always the motion picture center of the world, but it was far behind in major stage productions like those in New York and London—and that situation needed correction.

I encouraged eminent Eastern theater owners and producers to expand their operations to the West Coast. They were extremely reluctant because of problems previously encountered with unions in other cities.

Working closely with top management of Shubert Theaters I assured them that they would have the complete support of our union. We also offered to recommend that other West Coast musicians unions follow our lead, thus establishing a series of additional theatrical venues to offset the expense of bringing a large cast, sceneries, and props across the country.

Jerry Schoenfeld, Bernie Jacobs, and Phil Smith, heads of the Shubert organization, promptly began construction of the beautiful Shubert Theater in Century City. Soon major Broadway shows began successful runs in Los Angeles, previously considered a "poor theatrical area."

Shortly after the opening of the Shubert Theater, I had a call from Stan Seiden, who owned the small El Centro Theater in Hollywood. He told me that his friend Jimmy

Nederlander, one of the largest theater owners in the country, wanted to meet with me in New York.

Ida and I joined him at Club 21, where he told me that he was extremely interested in opening theaters in Hollywood and throughout the West Coast. He said, "Max, what potential union problems will I face there."

My response was, "Jimmy, we need your shows in Hollywood, and if you come, we will cooperate in every possible manner. We will waive the usual posting of cash bonds for you and will recommend that the other West Coast locals provide the same cooperation."

As a result of that meeting, Jimmy Nederlander eventually took over the Pantages Theater in Hollywood. It was built in the '30s as a stage theater for popular musicals and dramatic shows. In 1949, it was converted into a film house for R.K.O. Pictures by owner Howard Hughes.

In 1977, Nederlander completely renovated the beautiful art-deco palace to its former glory as a setting for touring stage productions. Ida and I were guests at the pre-opening party of Nederlander's first show, the New York Tony Award Winner, *Bubbling Brown Sugar.*

Ida said, "Jimmy, you have brought Broadway to Hollywood!" He liked her comment, and instructed his advertising department to use "Bringing Broadway to Hollywood!" in forthcoming publicity releases.

Nederlander soon expanded his California operation to include theaters in Orange County, San Diego, San Francisco, and Seattle. He appointed my friend Stan Seiden as his local manager. For many years, Local 47 enjoyed a good relationship with Nederlander's organization.

Since then, our musicians have worked at hundreds of additional jobs with top stage productions at the Shubert, the Pantages, and the Dorothy Chandler Pavilion, the Greek

Theater, the Wilshire Theater, the Henry Fonda Theater, etc.

I must have had the right formula, because all my theater contracts were promptly ratified by the musicians, there was never a strike, and my relationship with the Eastern producers developed into very warm friendships.

In addition to our important employment opportunities at that time in theaters, radio, TV, and film studios, Local 47 also had musicians working nightly in twelve hundred nightclubs, restaurants, and hotels. Those venues were their number-one source of income.

*   *   *

As president of Musicians Union Local 47 in Los Angeles, I always felt that the employers of our members were our friends. Many million-dollar contracts were results of a few sincere handshakes, and musicians went to work the next day. My negotiations were always overwhelmingly ratified by our members, although it often took months to complete the complicated contracts while the musicians were already on the job.

I established great relationships locally with many prominent people like the brilliant Lew Wasserman who developed Universal Studios into a worldwide attraction—and taught me the secret of negotiation.

I also worked closely with Nick Counter, head of the Motion Picture Producers Association, with Bob Franz of Capitol Records, and Jeff Katzenberg of Disney Studios. Members of Musicians Union Local 47 benefited from these important affiliations.

*   *   *

It was in the mid-'40s, during the Hollywood Musicians' revolt against policies instituted by American Federation of Musicians President Jimmy Petrillo. I was called to a private meeting with Henry Kaiser, General Council for the A.F. of M. There was a bitter labor war between us, and I was interested in what their chief attorney from Washington, D.C., had to say.

When I met Mr. Kaiser in his hotel suite in Los Angeles, I made it clear that, if our meeting was a gentlemanly exchange of views, I would stay. If, at any time, our discussion became an altercation, I would leave.

He quickly placated my concern by telling me that, as a youth, he studied the Talmud, the first written documentation defining civil and religious laws for the Jewish people.

Kaiser said, "Max, those secrets I learned from the Talmud taught me that fairness and compromise were more important than conflict. I always apply those ancient principles to my daily activity."

Our meeting progressed on a equitable basis and several areas were discussed. During my participation in many additional negotiations chaired by him, regardless of our differences, that Talmudic code of conduct was always in evidence; and many serious matters were amiably resolved.

I have never forgotten Lew Wasserman and Henry Kaiser. The wholesome morality of negotiation that I learned from them served me very well during my thirty years as a union official.

Ernest Fleischman, the Genius of the Hollywood Bowl and the Los Angeles Philharmonic

For years, Hollywood's reputation as a major entertainment center was primarily based on the film industry. Little was known of its additional cultural activities.

Under the expert guidance of the executive director Ernest Fleischman, the Los Angeles Philharmonic Orchestra rapidly developed into a first-class attraction.

When the acclaimed conductor Zubin Mehta was engaged to lead the ensemble, they worked together as a great team making the L.A. Philharmonic one of the premier orchestras in the world.

Their concerts consistently drew huge audiences to the Hollywood Bowl, which rapidly gained international popularity as an important musical venue. It became so popular that settlements in many Hollywood divorces involved contested custody of their revered box seats.

During Fleischman's regime, the Bowl, administered by the Philharmonic Association, was usually full—especially when major attractions were performing. Choice seats were often impossible to obtain unless one had season tickets. The boxes were all permanently occupied and bequeathed to family members through the years.

Ernest Fleischman made the Hollywood Bowl a very prominent summer attraction for residents and tourists. He knew what the people wanted—and gave it to them. He and I often discussed the importance of the Bowl as a site for family entertainment and a means of assuring future attendance—"continuity."

For many years, my wife Ida and I were model examples of "family" patronage. We had a seasonal box for all events in which we entertained many friends and business associates. Three generations of Hermans occupied that box.

On several occasions, we gave the seats to our daughter Marlene or our son Barry to entertain their friends. During the summer season, we felt it important that each of our grandchildren were given the box a few times to include their young friends. Our intention was to instill an interest in serious music that would continue over the years.

As Musicians Union President, I negotiated some of the best and fairest contracts in the nation with Fleischman. The participating musicians and the Philharmonic Association were always happy with the arrangements. Our close relationship became an outstanding accomplishment and was the subject of many published articles. I am extremely proud of those achievements. They could serve as examples of a perfect labor-management affiliation.

The orchestra's attorney, Dennis Vaughn, was also an extremely fair negotiator. He would have been another outstanding candidate for a seat on the U.S. Supreme Court.

Zubin Mehta gave me supreme compliments as a mediator and negotiator; he often said, "Max, I'm going to send you to Israel to help settle those severe middle-eastern problems!"

When plans were instituted to construct the new Walt Disney Concert Hall, Ernest Fleischman was involved in almost every aspect of this momentous structure—the new home for the L.A. Philharmonic Orchestra. He steadfastly kept the project moving through the many problems encountered along the way.

His astute supervision guided it from its initial concept, the brilliant contemporary design by famed architect Frank Gehry, to the most successful American concert hall opening since Tchaikovsky came to New York in 1891 to dedicate Carnegie Hall.

After that glamorous opening in October 2003, the Walt Disney Concert Hall has gained a world-wide reputation overcoming Boston's celebrated Symphony Hall and New York's Carnegie Hall that has reigned supreme for over a century.

A moderate area of the Walt Disney Concert Hall bears Fleischman's name, but it is lost amid the plethora of plaques recognizing corporate and donor contributions. For initiating the project and overcoming its many obstacles, he deserves better recognition.

The Los Angeles Philharmonic completed their first season in the Disney Hall, then continued playing their regular summer series at the Hollywood Bowl. I am sorry to say that the Hollywood Bowl's status as a major attraction changed considerably when the Philharmonic's Board of Directors did not renew Ernest Fleischman's contract. Attendance has fallen. Boxes are usually available—even on Saturday nights.

The Recording Musicians Association

I always had expert musicians on my negotiating teams. I believed that only the musicians working in various segments of the musical business, symphonies, films, TV, radio, theaters, recordings, etc., should participate in the ratification of contracts in their individual fields.

In 1972, a group of studio musicians in major U.S. and Canadian cities formed the Recording Musicians Association to assure effective representation during union contract negotiations that concerned them.

I favored the formation of the group. Since the recording musicians were experts in their field, and aware of the problems, they could help the A.F. of M. officers during negotiations with the record industry.

As president of Local 47 and a member of the International Executive Board, I met the recording musicians in New York to help with their organizational plans.

In January 1983, I retired after serving ten years as

president of Local 47. In recognition of my activity, I was honored by the governor and legislators of Rhode Island, my home state. They declared May 17, 1983 "Max Herman Day." Ida and I went to Providence to attend a banquet in my honor and I received a proclamation that now proudly hangs on my home office wall.

Back in the Saddle Again!

After enjoying seven years of retirement, I was visited by a group of the busiest musicians in the union led by Artie Kane and Dennis Dreath. They were all members of the Recording Musicians Association. Dennis later became the organization's national president.

They presented me with a petition signed by over 1000 members urging me to again run for President of Local 47 to unseat the current president, Bernie Fleischer, who had many disagreements with the RMA.

I discussed the situation with my wife and family. We decided that, since the petitioning members, who had supported my programs for many years, felt that the union needed help, I should comply with their request. I agreed to accept their nomination, and my name was added as a presidential candidate to the ballots being printed for the forthcoming election.

My slate of officers, Board of Directors, and Trial Board Members, received 74 percent of the vote—and I assumed the presidency for the second time.

Shortly after the election, I had a call from Marty Emerson, then President of the American Federation of Musicians. Marty was an outstanding president and a fine musician, a trombonist in many big bands including

Tommy Dorsey's. He informed me that our Local had filed a contentious lawsuit against the Disney Organization.

Disney's contract was with the A.F. of M., not Local 47, and the suit filed by the Local had no merit.

As a result, Disney no longer employed Local 47 musicians. They transferred all recording activity for their films, TV, and record label to foreign orchestras, depriving many of our members of lucrative jobs.

Marty's words to me were, "Max, you know everybody. Help us correct this bad situation. Meet with the Disney people. They won't talk to me, or our Washington attorney, or anyone from the A.F. of M."

Jeffrey Katzenberg, then a young Disney Vice-President, was the man to see. Since we had never met, I asked Nick Counter, President of the Motion Picture Association, and a good friend of Katzenberg, to accompany me during the meeting I had scheduled with him.

When we met, Nick said some very nice things about me to Katzenberg. My first words to him were: "Jeff, my union was absolutely wrong! And I am here to apologize!" He was astounded, and said, "But Max, you were not involved when this situation occurred!"

We continued our discussion for about twenty minutes and I repeatedly offered to solve whatever problems provoked the lawsuit. Finally, Katzenberg said, "Max, where have you been? And don't go away!"

I arranged for the suit to be dropped immediately, and the Hollywood musicians returned to their jobs at Disney Studio. I asked my vice president, Bill Peterson, to give me daily reports on the number of musicians being re-hired. In a very short time, over 500 Local 47 members were again employed by Disney.

Jeff Katzenberg and I became good friends and we continued working together during many negotiations that were usually quickly settled with a handshake. He later became president of the Disney firm, and currently is Chief Executive Officer of Dreamworks Animation with his partners Steven Spielberg and David Geffen.

Artie Kane and Dennis Dreath, who persuaded me to seek the union presidency again, became my staunchest supporters during my remaining years in office.

A Visit with the King

In about 1983, just before his annual overseas Christmas tour with Bob Hope to entertain U.S. servicemen, bandleader Les Brown told me that the King of Thailand had been very accommodating to his band during previous visits to Bangkok.

The King was born and raised in the U.S. where he learned to play the clarinet and eventually mastered a whole family of reed instruments. After his coronation, he frequently entertained American jazzmen and participated in jam sessions with them at his royal palace.

Bob Hope's tour was again scheduled to appear in Thailand to entertain U.S. troops stationed there, and Les asked if there was something they could present to the King in appreciation of his previous hospitality. I suggested we make him an Honorary Member of Local 47, Les liked the idea, and our Board of Directors voted to issue a gold card to His Highness.

A short time later, Bob Hope presented the Honorary Membership Card bearing my signature to the King who was very pleased with the gift. His name still appears on the Honorary Member page in our yearly directory, I sent him a copy, and he was very pleased.

A very memorable event occurred after I retired again

in 1993. Ida and I were booked on an Oriental tour that included a few days in Bangkok. She suggested that I write to the King and request a meeting during our stay.

We had no response to my letter until the evening before our tour departed from Los Angeles. A cablegram invited us to be the guests of His Royal Highness Brumibol Adulyadej in his palace home at 4:00 P.M. the afternoon of our arrival in Bangkok.

The driver who took us to the palace was surprised when the guards at the palace gate immediately waved us through when informed that Ida and I were the King's guests. A tall turbaned attendant took us to a large receiving hall and served us some orange juice. Soon a soldier in full dress uniform escorted us down a long hallway to an office door that opened automatically as we approached.

When we entered, we saw the King seated behind his desk. He rose, and shook Ida's hand, and said, "Welcome Mr. and Mrs. Herman." Photographers appeared and took our pictures with His Highness and promptly departed.

For about an hour and a half, the King and I discussed the many great musicians he admired including Benny Carter who was on my Board of Directors of Local 47. He knew a lot about jazz and enjoyed his visits with some of the world's finest musicians.

He invited me to return to play trumpet with him and his local group. It would have been a great honor, but our tour was soon departing, and I could not accept his invitation.

When it seemed appropriate for us to leave, I stood and thanked the King for his courtesy. Later Ida informed me that it was customary for guests to wait until their royal host excused them—but I said, "In my business you have to know when to get off!"

We were escorted back to our car and the chauffeur

was instructed to drive around the palace grounds before leaving. It was early evening, and we thought we saw elephants, tigers, and lions in the semi-darkness. They were actually shrubs expertly trimmed to appear lifelike.

Chapter Ten
Trumpet Royalty

In any creative field, to be great, an artist must have an individual style that is instantly recognizable. This axiom applies to actors, writers, graphic artists, sculptors, architects, designers, etc.—and especially trumpet players.

Throughout the history of jazz, these musicians, with only three valves at their disposal, perfected distinctive avenues of expression. The list is endless. For example:

Bix Beiderbecke achieved a melodic legato style. Charlie Spivak approached ballads with lyric clarity. Billy Butterfield played everything with tasteful perfection. Doc Severinsen was a technical wizard with a powerful sound and great interpretation skills. Harry James put his personal touch on lovely ballads and searing jazz.

Ziggy Elman was known for his Yiddish specialties and driving force. Jonah Jones' muted sounds were brilliant. Rex Stewart's remarkable half-valve technique was unforgettable. Raphael Mendez, and more recently, Bobby Rodriguez added a Salsa flavor to the trumpet's repertoire.

Sonny Dunham, Cat Anderson, and Maynard Ferguson were known for their high registers. When we talk about high registers, the great Tommy Stevenson, who played first trumpet in the early Jimmy Lunceford orchestra, was far ahead of his time.

*   *   *

I also salute trumpet colleagues who made the Golden Era of the Big Bands a memorable one: Andy Ferretti, Pee Wee Irwin, Zeke Zarchy, Chris Griffin, Ralph Muzzillo, Bobby Jones, Roy Eldrige, Jimmy Campbell, Bobby Guy, Snooky Young, Stewart Grow, Bobby Bryant, Steve Lipkin, Graham Young, Lyman Vunk, Eddie Wade, Dave Wade, Holly Humphries, Ray Nance, Al Aaron, Art DePew, Mannie Stevens, and Buddy Childers.

I would be remiss if I didn't mention personal friends who helped create an industry: Bunny Berigan, Teddy Buckner, Harry "Sweets" Edison, Bobby Goodrich, Dave Frankel, Gerald Wilson, John Best, and the King of them all, the man who played beautifully until he died—Louis Armstrong.

We must not overlook the great trumpet players heard in motion pictures, on TV and radio, and on commercial recordings: First, my friend who could do it all in every field—Mannie Klein. Charlie Margolis played first trumpet during many radio and TV broadcasts from New York. His trumpet solo on Eddie Fisher's hit RCA Victor record in 1954, *Oh, My Papa*, was not credited on the label, but it contributed greatly to the record's success.

Uan Rasey is noted for his stellar trumpet work on the great motion picture score of *An American in Paris*. Eddie Ehlert was rarely identified, but he was the wonderful muted trumpet soloist often heard with Bing Crosby.

Radio, TV, and movie credits seldom mention these masterful trumpet players heard on hundreds of programs and films: Ruby Weinstein, Mannie Weinstock, Claude Gordon, Frank Zinzer, George Wendt, Frank Beach, Gene Lafreniere, Joe Triscari, John Audino, Charlie Griffith, John Clyman, Bob O'Donnell, Chase Craig, Irving Bush, Charlie

Davis, Tony Terran, Warren Luening, Mannie Stevens, Chuck Finley, Maury Harris, Cecil Read, Clyde Resinger, Tommy Stevens, George Werth, Malcolm McNabb, Rick Baptist, and George Graham.

The following group of noteworthy trumpet teachers certainly should be included in this category: Max Schlossberg, Uan Rasey, Walter Smith Sr., Del Staigers, Louis Maggio, Harry Glantz, Frank Simon, Herbert Clark, Sol Castin, Harold Mitchell, Dave Grupp, and my wonderful teacher, Alexander Billincoff in Providence, who, by 1942, had fifty students.

I would be remiss if I did not mention the New Orleans trumpet star Wynton Marsalis, a marvel of the current generation of jazz greats. He can play any style with ease—from authentic New Orleans jazz, to music of the contemporary era, to classical material. I have not had the pleasure of meeting Wynton, but his name belongs in any compendium of accomplished trumpet players.

I am probably overlooking some additional important members of this "Trumpet Royalty" group, and I apologize for any that have been carelessly omitted.

Mannie Klein

"Mannie was a generous kind human being. I think of all the musicians he helped, all their trumpets he got out of hock . . . all the musicians who stayed at his house when they were broke . . . all the jobs he got for his friends.
"He was the most unprejudiced person in the world, and fought so hard for everyone to be treated equally."
—Joan McInerny, nurse who cared for Mannie Klein during his last months.

Mannie Klein was born in 1908 on the Lower East Side of New York City. He was playing professionally at the age of sixteen. He was probably the best versatile trumpet player who ever lived. He studied with trumpet teacher Max Schlossberg for ten years, beginning at age six. Mannie's parents were very poor, and often were unable to pay for the lessons. He never forgot his teacher, and in later years, sent him money almost every week.

Mannie could play first trumpet in a symphony, first or jazz trumpet in big bands, and was equally proficient in studio orchestras, Latin bands, Hawaiian bands, Klezmer bands, Dixieland bands, and as a brass band soloist.

At one time, during the radio days in New York, Mannie played on nineteen programs every week. On some, he sent substitutes to rehearsals, and he played the shows expertly reading the intricate scores "cold." Many record companies wanted him, and he recorded under various pseudonyms.

During his long career, Mannie played in Carnegie Hall, and in bands led by Glenn Miller, Benny Goodman, and Tommy Dorsey, and on scores of film soundtracks—including the memorable "Taps" sequence in *From Here to Eternity.* He carefully coached the film's star Montgomery Clift, who expertly handled the horn on the screen while Mannie's tones were heard on the soundtrack.

Mannie had a heart of gold and helped many trumpet players including me, as I reported earlier. When Ziggy Elman was no longer able to play as well as he did in the past, Mannie helped him earn some needed money. This occurred during the recording for the film, *The Benny Goodman Story* in 1955. Mannie played Ziggy's famous solo on *And the Angels Sing,* and arranged for Ziggy to receive screen credit and the recording fee. Again, when

Claude Gordon, a fine trumpet player at CBS became ill, Mannie played—and Claude got the check.

Mannie always supported my efforts as a Union official, and helped me in all my election campaigns. When he died in 1994, I wrote the following tribute that was published in Local 47's monthly "Overture":

"The person who coined the phrase 'a star among the superstars' must have had Mannie Klein in mind—both as an artist and as a human being. Many of us credit our success to his unselfish help. He was a legend and will never be replaced. We loved him."

Mannie Klein and Uan Rasey Blow Their Horns at the Olympic Games in Japan

Mannie Klein and Uan Rasey, both great trumpet stars and sports enthusiasts, were fans at the 1964 Olympic Games held in Tokyo, Japan. They became very annoyed whenever the Japanese band played our national anthem because only the first eight bars were played.

Since this was the first time the games were held in Japan after their defeat in World War II, Mannie and Uan felt that a more respectful rendition of the "Star Spangled Banner" seemed appropriate.

The Olympic Stadium was sold-out on the games' final day. When the U.S. athletes were presented with their medals, and the band again played just the first part of the anthem, Mannie and Uan took out their pocket trumpets, and stood up. With Mannie playing the harmony and Uan providing the melody, they continued the number to its conclusion while 100,000 people applauded. The event was covered by sports photographers, newsreel cameramen, and international network television. Coverage of their musical expression of national pride received world-wide attention.

A few months later, Ida and I attended a party celebrating the birthday of the great drummer Sammy Weiss. As we entered, we heard a small band, and Mannie was on the stand—playing his little pocket trumpet.

Noticing our arrival, Mannie announced, "Here comes our president! He's not only a great president, he's also a great trumpet player!" He invited me to sit-in with the band, handed me his small horn, and sat with Ida while I played.

She told Mannie that she would like to find a horn like that to give me for my birthday. A few months later, when I unwrapped her gift, the horn that Mannie played in Japan was in the box—his special gift to me!

Raphael Mendez

Raphael Mendez was a superb trumpet soloist, a great technician, a good friend, and, above all, a fine gentleman.

He recorded many complex violin selections that included a four-minute circular breathing version of Paganinni's torrid "Perpetual Motion."

He concluded the sixteenth-note exercise triumphantly on high F# without taking a break—an unheard of achievement!

Raphael and I shared first trumpet parts on recordings we made in 1945 with Al Sachs' orchestra. We were among a dozen trumpet players invited as guests to a party hosted by a trumpet manufacturer (Benge) to evaluate their new instruments.

They asked me to play the Bob Crosby theme, "Summertime," without any accompaniment. When I finished,

Raphael loudly exclaimed, "Max, you sure batted them out!" I was astonished to hear him use the identical phrase that Glenn Miller used about seven years earlier when he heard me at the Roseland Ballroom with Joe Haymes' band.

Chapter Eleven
Music As a Career and an Art

Being a professional musician is a very self-rewarding occupation; but lately, making a good living at it has become increasingly difficult. For many years, the American Federation of Musicians of the U.S. and Canada had over 330,000 members. Today, the rosters list under 100,000 members.

New York City, once the center of employment for musicians, had 32,000 members in Musicians Union Local 802 before World War II. Today, they have less than 10,000 members.

During music's "Golden Era," until the mid-40s, dining and dancing was the number-one recreation activity for people of many countries. In the United States, almost every hotel had live music for dancing and dining every day of the week. Some hotels booked well-known traveling bands, but most of them featured local musicians that earned from $80.00 to $100.00 a week.

The local radio stations had staff orchestras of twelve to fifteen musicians. Network radio programs and motion picture studios employed orchestras from fifteen to seventy-five musicians. Our great film studio musicians could score a complete picture in three hours with very few second "takes." It takes a foreign orchestra much longer—but it costs the film companies a great deal less!

The nation's big music centers were New York and Chicago. Dance halls were in every city. A dozen major ballrooms flourished in the Los Angeles area. Radio broadcasts were live from all areas of the country. Musicians had an opportunity to hone their skills playing nightly in all these bands. Unfortunately, that valuable learning experience is no longer available to today's young musicians.

Paul Whiteman was the first bandleader to pay lofty wages for his stellar musicians. As early as 1928, the weekly payroll for his thirty-five-piece orchestra exceeded $7,000.00, an average of about $200.00 per musician. The highest-paid member, arranger Ferde Grofé, received $375.00. Bing Crosby's pay was $150.00. Bix Beiderbecke's weekly check was $200.00.

During the peak years of the Big Band Era, hundreds of bands toured the country bringing their popular "swing" music to large and small cities from coast to coast. The musicians were well paid, especially those in the top bands like Benny Goodman, the Dorseys, Artie Shaw, Guy Lombardo, Horace Heidt, Bob Crosby, etc.

Basic pay ranged from $125.00 to $200.00 a week. Some featured artists made more. To my knowledge, the highest figure, $500.00 a week, was Ziggy Elman's weekly wage while he led Tommy Dorsey's band during the leader's illness.

We were responsible for our own expenses on the road—clothing, laundry, food, and lodging. Hotels along the way catered to traveling bands and rooms were available for two or three dollars a night, double occupancy. (The highest we paid was $5.00 at the swank new Rice Hotel in Houston!)

We received additional pay for record dates, TV, and motion picture performances based on the negotiated contracts with the American Federation of Musicians.

After World War II, Las Vegas became the music center of the United States. Over 90 percent of the local musicians were employed. I am sorry to say that now Las Vegas is almost a ghost town for live music. Even the big productions are using recorded music—usually taped in Europe! The same can be said for the nation's many studios, theaters, and nightclubs.

The symphonies in this country are still a great source for employment of musicians but they are also having financial problems.

My "Dream" Band

Friends often ask me to create a mythical "dream band" assembled from the many musicians I have played with. It would be great to hear these great musicians playing together:

Trumpets: Billy Butterfield, Bunny Berigan, and
    Charlie Spivak
Reeds: Eddie Miller, Tenor sax; "Doc" Rando, Alto sax;
    Gus Bivona, Clarinet
Trombone: Buddy Morrow
Piano: Johnny Guarnieri
Bass: Arthur "Doc" Goldberg
Guitar: Tony Mottola
Drums: Nick Fatool

Chapter Twelve
Race and Religious Harmony

Any success I have had as a working musician or as a union leader can be attributed to my personal creed:

All musicians—arrangers, sidemen, and leaders, should be treated equally. I don't care where you come from. I don't care if you are a woman or a man, young or old. Your race or religion does not matter. If you are a musician or a singer, you are part of my family.

As a Jew, growing up in a predominantly Gentile North Providence, R.I., I did not experience any religious bias. Although I was a political, social, athletic, and musical manager in my home town, there was no indication of bigotry.

My parents never spoke about anti-Semitism in Russia; my father came to the U.S. to avoid military service. The families of my mother and father came here because of economical opportunities not available in the old country.

Throughout my personal and professional life, I was never aware of any anti-Semitism perhaps because of the manner in which I treated those with whom I came in contact. This applied to my years as a member of several bands, and as the first Jewish president of the Hollywood Musicians Union. I was a highly respected publisher of Christian Evangelical music, and worked closely with many Christian composers and bandleaders.

Jazz musicians, and most fans, are strongly united behind the music they love, and are not separated by race or religion. As early as 1923, the great New Orleans Rhythm Kings, a very popular white band, featured Jelly Roll Morton in the first racially mixed recording session that produced several historically important recordings.

Despite the cruel segregation laws that existed in New Orleans years ago, the black and white musicians surreptitiously played side by side. They also broke another color barrier in 1929 when Sidney Arodin, a white clarinetist, recorded with Jones-Collins Hot 8—the first racially mixed recordings made in New Orleans.

When I was in the Joe Haymes band, we were frequently booked on joint tours with the great black orchestra led by Jimmie Lunceford. We often participated in a "Battle of Bands" with them at the Roseland Ballroom on Broadway at the Savoy Ballroom in Harlem.

Walking down 125th Street carrying my trumpet case, I was always warmly greeted by black musicians and the public. During the 1939 New York World's Fair, the Bob Crosby band was featured in a "Cavalcade of Bands" with seven or eight groups, black and white, alternating day and night. We had a mutual respect for each other and many enduring friendships developed.

Although the personnel of a sixteen-piece band like Bob Crosby's included a cross section of religious affiliations, we always got along very well together.

When I first joined Crosby, Joseph Kearney was the band's manager and had been there for several years. He was a devout Catholic. Joseph was apparently an orphan raised by nuns and missionary clergymen. He left us to be ordained as a priest.

The band attended his ordination ceremony at St. Vibiano Cathedral in Los Angeles. As is customary, after the ceremony, the new priests stood at the altar to bless their families. I knew that "Father Joe" had no family, so I went to the altar for the first blessing. The rest of the band followed us to the altar. I will never forget the broad smile on Father Joe's face.

I played with Redd Harper in the Coast Guard Band. Before the war, he sang and played trumpet with Jimmy Grier at the Biltmore Hotel in Los Angeles. After the War, he became a Protestant Evangelical Minister associated with Billy Graham, and starred in Graham's films.

At my son Barry's bar mitzvah, Father Joe and Reverend Redd Harper attended the ritual. They both were also at my daughter's wedding. After the ceremony, they joined the receiving line and each hugged and kissed Marlene, Ida and me. Our friends were impressed with the knowledge that a rabbi, a priest, and a minister blessed Marlene's marriage!

In the early 1970s, Los Angeles Mayor Tom Bradley met with me in my Local 47 office to discuss a serious problem that existed between Latino and black students—and their violent street gangs that were almost impossible to control.

To address this problem, I assembled the Black and Brown Brotherhood Jazz Band co-led by Eddie Cano, a popular Latino pianist, and Buddy Collette, a highly acclaimed black reed artist. They selected the best Latino and black musicians including Oscar Brashear, Britt Woodman, Ruben Leon, Pancho Sanchez, and David Trancosa. The Mayor arranged for performances in many schools that had serious problems.

The opposing factions sat side-by-side enjoying jazz music played by the racially mixed orchestra. At the conclusion of each concert, the students in the audience stood and shouted their enthusiastic approval—proving that music can be a unifying experience to a young audience.

When invited to come on the stage and talk to the musicians, they realized it was possible for these artists to play good music together despite their disparate racial backgrounds.

The results of these sessions were like magic! The musicians, paid by the recording industry and the American Federation of Musicians Trust Fund, achieved what the teachers, police, and city leaders were unable to accomplish!

I asked Mayor Bradley and Chief of Police Darryl Gates to barricade specific intersections where gang crimes prevailed, and set up portable bandstands and provide a piano. We sent our best bands to play for street dances in different areas each week. We urged the cops to stay away, and gang leaders complied with our request to police themselves.

There was never a bad incident during the school concerts or the street dances, and the racial gang warfare abated considerably.

A few decades later, I formed the Sisterhood and Brotherhood All-Star Jazz Band under the direction of Buddy Collette. We proved that a combination of fine players of both genders and many races could successfully blend their talents. The first event, a free concert, at Cal States' Luckman Auditorium, was so successful that I was able to obtain financing from the Motion Picture Trust Fund for a series of successful concerts in the high schools.

I was happy to learn, that, as a result of our success, the City of Long Beach also launched a series of concerts in their schools. Hopefully, cities around the country with similar problems will create comparable musical programs to combat the difficulties.

The late Benny Carter, among jazz's most highly respected artists, served on my Union Board of Directors for two years. He often told me, "Max, I will never forget what you have done for my people."

I have always treasured Benny's words since they pertain to my unbiased selection of black colleagues, whose wisdom I respected, and in whom I placed my trust for guidance regarding important decisions.

Nellie Lutcher and Buddy Collette were on my Board of Directors. Elmer Fain, Jimmie Clark, and the great Duke Ellington trombonist Lawrence Brown were my Business Agents.

Marl Young, the first black officer of a major musician's union, always accompanied me as a delegate to the American Federation of Musicians yearly convention. He holds a record of being our members' first choice among twenty-one candidates to represent the Federation at A.F.L./C.I.O. conventions.

After my retirement, I helped produce a series of highly acclaimed musical reviews that combined the talents of black and white, salsa, and klezmer musicians.

Klezmer, in Yiddish, is short for "klei zemer" (musical instruments). It refers to the ancient combination of Greek and Central/Eastern European music originally played for dancers at Jewish weddings.

The early klezmer musicians and the Jewish cantors had something in common—improvisation. The introspective cantorial chants are still personal interpretations of ancient prayers in the Torah—just as the jazz musicians interpret melodies in their individual style. The bright toe-tapping/hand-clapping rhythm of klezmer music is currently enjoying a brisk revival on the international jazz scene.

My friend Berle Adams, head of the Arts Council of the University of Judaism, created the concept of our racially mixed musical reviews. He chose the stars, and wrote the script for my shows. He asked me to select the musicians and to research some of the klezmer music that was popular years ago.

In our blend of musical cultures, we presented an ethnic mix combining Yiddish folk songs with Latin jazz and popular American standards. These concert performances in 1997 epitomized the value of jazz at a conduit to racial harmony.

Herb Jeffries MC'd with charming grace, and evoked tearful response when he sang "Eli, Eli" in Yiddish. Rifka Seiden, an outstanding singer of Jewish songs, was also featured.

I paired Latin trumpet star Bobby Rodriguez with Judy Fox, Cantor of the Synagogue for the Performing Arts, doing a duet on "My Yiddisha Mama." We had an extraordinary Black-Italian-Jewish trio with Buddy Collette on flute, Al Viola playing guitar, and Richard Simon, on string bass. They played sentimental Jewish folk melodies on a darkened stage lit only by a purple spotlight. There was not a dry eye in the auditorium!

Our all-star bands, black and white, Jewish and Gentile, led by clarinetist Abe Most and Bobby Rodriguez, also included Sam Most, famed klezmer clarinetist Leo Chelyapov, and Zeke Zarchy, Al Aarons, Allen Weiss, Art Depew, Hershey Bell, Snooky Young, Tony Giaimo, Ray Sherman, and Gerald Wiggins.

They featured popular tunes, like "Bei Mir Bist Du Schoen," that are based on traditional Yiddish melodies. Each was cleverly arranged in three forms—a chorus as a ballad, another in a jazz mode, and, finally, in klezmer style.

Every performance was sold out. All the musicians were paid, but Berle Adams and I contributed our services to the University of Judaism Arts Council.

The Help Youth Charities Group

After World War II, when the big band era faded, Hollywood offered a variety of employment opportunities in the entertainment field. As a result, many moved west to seek studio employment in the thriving motion pictures field, phonograph records, radio, and soon, the television industry.

We were here in a strange new environment with our families and gradually gravitated toward others with similar situations and backgrounds many of whom we knew during our earlier activities in the east. Eventually a group of prominent Jewish members of the entertainment and business fields formed an informal club to celebrate our social and family events together.

We decided that we should do some charity work, and named our organization "The Help Youth Charities Group." That was over half a century ago, and we are still functioning. We currently have about 50 active members who continue to provide a valuable service to the community.

I would like to acknowledge some of the people I have enjoyed working with as we formulated the goals and aspirations of The Help Youth Charities Group.

George Wyle, was the musical conductor for the Andy Williams, Alan Young, and Nanette Fabrey shows, and the composer of the *Gilligan's Island* theme and the hit holiday tune, "It's the Most Wonderful Time of the Year."

Ticker Freeman was Dinah Shore's accompanist. Bandleader George Wald was the music copyist for many radio, motion picture, and TV scores. Sammy Friedman and Sid Goldstein were prominent song pluggers. Bill Rinehart was an investment banker. Jess Schneier and his brother Eddie, owned a chain of drug stores, and Harry Bluhm owned a food market and liquor store.

The group also included jeweler Rowan Klein, furrier Arnold Z. Arnold, businessman Irving Adeleman, garment manufacturer Irving Hindus, and musician, Julie Losch.

Each year, the Help Youth Charities Group has raised $50,000.00 to $60,000.00 through donations and various fund-raising events, including annual golf tournaments. Featured artists have been: Jerry Lewis, Billy Daniels, Herb Jeffries, and many illustrious guest stars. We have very little overhead expenses and none of our members receive any compensation. All profits are donated to deserving handicapped children.

Chapter Thirteen
Memories of My Colleagues

There are many interesting stories about people in the music business that seldom appear in print. Here are a few that come to mind:

Berle Adams: A Super Executive—
A Sucker for Talent

Much more should be said about Berle Adams, my collaborator on the University of Judaism shows. I have known this gifted man since I joined the Bob Crosby band in 1939 when he was booking them. As a super executive, his many achievements could fill a book—in fact, they did! In 1995 he wrote, *A Sucker for Talent, from Cocktail Lounges to MCA: 50 Years as Agent, Manager, and Executive.* Its 300 pages, in a second edition in 1998, delineate most of his creative skills.

As a very young man, Berle had a keen eye and an ear for discovering new talent and, as an agent, he developed their careers and created major stars like Louis Jordan, with whom he was associated for many years. He arranged for artists' bookings in cocktail lounges, he booked orchestras in one-night stands and tours, and became the agent for such diverse entertainers as: Ethel Merman, Dinah Shore,

Frankie Laine, Fred Astaire, Jerry Lewis, Danny Kaye, Rosemary Clooney, Jack Benny, and Gene Kelly.

Berle also produced films, founded a publishing firm, launched an independent company, Mercury Records, to record hits by the artists he managed, and created a pioneering international distribution company for MCA television programs. As Vice President of the William Morris Agency, he became one of the first great agents for athletic stars in football, baseball, and basketball.

At eighty-nine, he is still active with his own television distribution firm, and provides support and leadership to several cancer research organizations. It is an accepted fact, if a worthy project is in need of guidance or promotion, somebody will say, "Call Berle Adams!"

Earl Williams
Serena Kay Williams

Earl Williams and his Orchestra was an important Los Angeles party band in the days before disc jockeys with turntables and stacks of records replaced live orchestras at private functions. Earl played tenor sax and his wife Serena sang, played bass, and expertly handled the M.C. chores. They entertained at many parties that Ida and I had for our family and my "Help Youth Charities Group."

Earl and Serena actively supported me when I was a candidate in Union elections. When I became president, I appointed Earl as an assistant. He worked at my side throughout my years in office.

Serena Kay Williams has been an active member of Local 47 since its first day in January 1950. To my knowledge she has not missed a single meeting. When an opening occurred on the Board of Directors in 1977, Serena was nominated and won by a large majority.

I valued her knowledge and wisdom during her period on the Board. In 1985, she became the first female titled officer as Secretary of the Union, and has served in the capacity continually. I feel that Serena will break all records for years of service as a incumbent titled officer.

In addition to her secretarial chores, she expertly edits "Overture," Local 47's popular monthly publication. She was honored by the National Sheet Music Society in 1996 for her "contribution to the American Musical Heritage through her efforts on behalf of performing musicians." A year later the Los Angeles City Council recognized her contributions to society and the field of music.

Speaking for all members of the Union, I salute Serena Kay and Earl Williams for their dedicated service to the organization.

Trombonist Abe Lincoln

Abram ("Abe") Lincoln was a great trombonist—and a happy-go-lucky character. His humorous escapades could fill a book. We worked together in many studio orchestras in the early '40s.

He was among those few jazz greats whose extended careers thrived during the Jazz Age, the Swing Era, the Dixieland Revival, and continued until his death in 2000 at ninety-three.

It is interesting to note that he played with Red Nichols in New York City in 1925 at the peak of the Jazz Era; three decades later, he resumed his relationship with Nichols in Los Angeles adding impetus to the surging Traditional Jazz Revival movement that is still in progress.

Lincoln was also a member of a select group of influential artists, highly admired by fellow musicians, who have eluded the attention of the average jazz fan. His name has appeared only briefly in most source material, usually referring to his sideman activities with noted leaders. Few publications have printed major articles depicting his elaborate career.

Abe gracefully avoided questions regarding his unique name and an apocryphal tale that has been told and re-told by musicians and fans over the years. The often repeated episode is probably the best "musician's" story in jazz history.

He vehemently denied the validity of many variations that have perpetuated the legendary saga. The story, apparently only partially based on a factual incident, is so very appropriate, it should be included here. This is one of the many variations:

It seems that Abe and another noted trombonist were stopped for a traffic violation while driving home after a job.

The police officer grimly asked Abe, the driver, "What's your name?"

"I'm Abe Lincoln," he replied.

The officer, obviously annoyed, said, "O.K., wise guy, I guess your buddy there is George Washington!"

Abe answered, "As a matter of fact—this IS George Washington."

His companion was a highly respected former member of orchestras led by Don Redman, Benny Carter, Fletcher Henderson, and Louis Armstrong. George Washington was his legal name.

The officer immediately placed the two musicians under arrest and escorted them to the Police Station where they were booked for drunk driving. After presenting their identifications, the officer apologetically offered them a cup of coffee, and they were released.

"That's old stuff," Abe told my friend, Floyd Levin, the jazz journalist who helped me on this project. "I don't talk about it anymore. They've dogged me about that story for years. It never happened!"

Dave Frankel

I met Dave Frankel when I joined Joe Haymes' band in 1936. He was an outstanding trumpet player, and got his big start earlier with Van Alexander's orchestra.

Dave was a fine musician, well educated, and a very bright man, but he had a strange attitude. He accepted many lucrative jobs, but only played to his best ability if he liked the leader. He liked Joe Haymes, and he liked Van Alexander.

When Dave worked for Tommy Dorsey, and later Gus Arnheim and Vic Schoen, conductor for the Andrews Sisters, he played very well during ensembles, but, when it came to playing his hot jazz solos, he just sat there without blowing a note! That is probably why he did not keep those jobs very long!

Van Alexander

As a very young man in New York, before forming his own orchestra, Alexander Feldman wrote arrangements for orchestra leader Chick Webb. In 1936, he arranged many numbers that Ella Fitzgerald recorded with Webb's band. He collaborated with her on "A-Tisket A-Tasket," one of the biggest hits of the era. Decca sold 250,000 copies of the recording in just a few months. Composer credits on the Decca Record appeared as "Fitzgerald/Feldman."

A few years later, he was encouraged by Eli Oberstein, RCA Victor's recording director, to organize his own band.

"Oberstein was responsible for changing my name," he told Floyd Levin during an interview a few years ago. "He thought 'Alexander Feldman and his Orchestra' didn't sound professional, and asked me, 'What's your middle name?' I said, 'Van Vliet, after my mother's mother name.' He said, 'There's your name! Take the Van from your middle name and add your ALEXANDER'—and that's how 'Al Feldman' became 'Van Alexander'—legally, in court since 1938."

Van Alexander led a very popular East Coast band before moving to California in 1943. He eventually became highly successful as an arranger-conductor on radio, TV, and motion pictures. Van is still an extremely important member of local 47.

George Wyle

I met Bernie Weisman when I first came to New York in the late '30s. He was the pianist and arranger for many local bands and later arranged and played piano for Olson and Johnson's hit Broadway review, *Hellzapoppin*. Our paths seldom crossed again since I was traveling with the bands and he was stationed in Manhattan.

Several years later, after I became established as a Hollywood studio musician, I had a all from contractor Dave Klein to play first trumpet in George Wyle's Orchestra on the Alan Young NBC radio show.

When I entered the studio for the first rehearsal, the

leader, George Wyle, turned out to be my old friend Bernie Weisman. Like in Van Alexander's case, it was customary then for professional people to change their names to avoid discrimination by employers and fans. We had a wonderful reunion and I occupied George Wyle's first trumpet chair until I became a union official.

George later arranged and conducted for several major stars including Andy Williams, Nanette Fabrey, Howard Keel, and many others. He wrote the TV theme for *Gilligan's Island*, and "It's the Most Wonderful Time of the Year," played during the NFL 2003 play-off games and the Super Bowl.

Muggsy Spanier

Muggsy Spanier lost the little finger on his right hand during a childhood accident. A review of one of our performances appeared in a Detroit newspaper. It said, "Mr. Spanier can play more cornet with four fingers than most players can with five!"

* * *

This country has had, and still has, some of the greatest, and most influential musicians in the world. It would be impossible to include all of them here. I can recall many additional episodes involving my colleagues that have never been revealed; here are a few more:

Wingy Manone's wife disappeared shortly after their baby was born. Wingy took the infant with him on all his jobs, and between sets, took care of the baby in a little basket.

A violin player in Rudy Vallee's orchestra became ill and was confined to a hospital for the rest of his life. Rudy paid him his salary until he died many years later. When Joe Ross, Frank Sinatra's music copyist, needed costly elaborate dental work, Frank Sinatra paid the bill.

Mickey Katz was a veteran of the Spike Jones' City Slickers. When I played with the famed Yiddish dialect clarinetist-comedian, he was starring in his long-running Los Angeles stage production, *Borschtcapades*. His teenage son, Joel Grey, sang and danced in the show, and recorded a Capitol LP, "Songs My Father Taught Me." Joel, of course, later became famous for his wonderful role in *Cabaret*.

Arthur "Doc" Goldberg, the great bass player with whom I worked in the Hudson-DeLange and George Hall bands, who later went with Glenn Miller, was not an M.D. He had no medical training. But he always had a doctor's bag full of pharmaceuticals that came in handy every day. When we needed an aspirin, a Tums, or a Band-Aid, "Doc" was always there.

All bands had girl singers, and the musicians I worked with treated them as their little sisters. Doris Day, Gloria DeHaven, and several others who sang with the bands, later became movie stars.

During the Big Band Era, we always traveled by bus. Often, during a series of "one-nighters," we had to sleep while enroute to the next job. We were unable to have our clothes laundered until we reached a longer engagement. In the summertime, before air conditioning, we suffered greatly in the hot bus. Occasionally, when we passed a river, we would stop the bus, and jump in the cool water—nude!

The Bob Crosby band was very popular in Chicago. We made several appearances at the famed Blackhawk Restaurant where jazz bands had appeared since the '20s. During one of these engagements, Irving Fazola and our drummer Ray Bauduc exchanged some bitter words on the bandstand. Their discussion became more heated during the intermission and it appeared that fists would begin flying.

"Faz" made the first move and I jumped on his back in an attempt to hold him back. Remember, I weighed only 118 pounds, and the huge clarinetist topped 280! He whirled around to disengage my grasp and it felt like I was on a merry-go-round! A few blows were exchanged and soon the skirmish ended. They shook hands and the encounter was soon forgotten. But I have always remembered that dizzying flight on Irving Fazola's back!

I am reminded of the "Czar," James Caesar Petrillo, who was President of the American Federation of Musicians for many years. He was the greatest speaker and M.C. I ever heard. When he spoke, everybody listened. He had a great trick. He would use street talk when necessary, and spoke like a college president when he thought it was appropriate. He was investigated twice by Congress and each time they ended up applauding him.

While I strongly opposed his approach to union politics, I respected his position, and refrained from using unpleasant admonitions. He was a brilliant leader and the architect of the music performance trust funds that have sponsored thousands of free concerts in schools, hospitals, parks, senior citizens' homes, etc. Musicians received payment from union royalties on phonograph record sales.

He also fathered the residual payment policy that has been a great benefit to our members. Petrillo held dictatorial powers over the A.F. of M. membership and adopted many laws that the Hollywood musicians were against.

After he sadly lost a young son due to a serious germ infection, he would never shake hands with anyone—he extended a pinky finger. He made an exception with my wife, Ida, who he liked very much, and always shook her hand.

After our political battles were over, Jimmy and I became good friends. He always complimented me on my presidential activities and urged me to become a member of the American Federation of Musicians Executive Board. With his support, I was elected, and served on the Executive Board for several years.

Dr. Thomas W. Wing

My good friend, Dr. Wing, is an electronics genius, a super herbologist, and an amazing diagnostician. His electronic acupuncture machine is among the many body-healing devices he has invented. Ida and I have benefited from his great skills for over half a century, and we attribute our good health today to his guidance.

Over the years, our relationship with Thomas and his wife, Kay, warmed into a close friendship and we have attended many of each other's family events. Kay, unfortunately died recently, but we are still in close touch with Thomas. He and I have lunch together frequently.

Epilogue

After I retired from the union in 1993, I received several lucrative employment offers. Jimmy Nederlander offered me the position of West Coast Chief Negotiator for his company at a six-figure annual salary with generous expense allowances including travel cost that included Ida.

I also received proposals of executive positions in the film industry, and officers of several musicians unions offered to support me as a candidate for president of the American Federation of Musicians of the U.S.A. and Canada.

Although those offers were all very flattering, I thanked everyone and declined. I just wanted to do what I wanted, when I wanted, and to enjoy my wonderful family.

Ida and I have been happily married for sixty-four years, and we are proud of our children, grandchildren, and great-grandchildren. We have been able to build a large house and send our son Barry to University of Southern California Dental School for eight years. He is now a practicing dentist and he and his wife Sharon have a daughter, Abbey, who is married to Jason Meshecow.

Our daughter Marlene was married to Warren Seltzer and they have three children. Allison, Stephanie, and Michael—and Stephanie has a son, Landon. Marlene is now an attorney. When she had been married twenty-five years, with three children, she decided to study law, and went to night school for five years. Marlene was among the eight in her class of forty that graduated and she passed the bar exam the first time she took it. She now has a successful practice specializing in Elder Law and has helped many of her clients. Our granddaughter Allison is married to Commander Chris Tomney of the Coast Guard, and they have two children, Katie and Zachery.

While writing this material, I celebrated my ninetieth birthday. I started to play golf after I was seventy-five years old. I now play eighteen holes every week with Norman Brown and a group of my peers and eighteen holes with my son Barry and his friends. I made my first "eagle" on my eighty-eighth birthday on July 1, 2002.

Over the years, as a member of the Braemar Country Club in Tarzana, California, I have "birdied" every hole at each of the two courses. I have shot better than my age four or five times—(each year it gets easier!)

A few months after my 90th birthday, just before completing this book, I hit my first hole-in-one! It was on the 155-yard eighth hole at Braemar's East Course—on November 12, 2004, a date I will always remember.

A Closing Memory:

In the early '40s, shortly after I joined the Bob Crosby orchestra, I received a call from the mayor of my hometown, North Providence, Rhode Island. He said the city officials would like to meet with me the next time I visited my family. A few months later, the band was playing some one-nighters in New England including a date in Providence. I was invited to meet with the mayor, chief of police, the highway commissioner, and the city tax assessor.

Since I had been successful earlier as their campaign manager, they wanted me to return to Rhode Island and assist them with several political problems. They offered to buy a very popular Providence hotel, make me a 50 percent owner and manager at a very good salary, and again run their campaigns.

I thanked them for the generous offer, but turned them down since I had finally achieved my goal playing first trumpet with the Crosby orchestra and sitting in the chair previously occupied by my idol, Charlie Spivak.

Musicians are seldom clever businessmen, and I was no exception. That hotel is still one of the most popular in town and is now worth several million dollars. But I have no regrets!

I am proud of the role I played during the great Big Band Era and my efforts that altered the course of the American Federation of Musicians, created our great Pension Fund, the Special Payments Fund, and the formation of the Recording Musicians Association.

When I retired, I was voted A.F. of M. Executive Board Member Emeritus at their national convention, and Local 47 voted me President Emeritus. My life has been very fulfilling. I look back with pride on wonderful experiences and accomplishments as a working musician, and as a union official.

Musicians are wonderful people, and I am glad to say that I will always be one of them!

I welcome this opportunity to share some of my memories with you.

—Max Herman, December 20, 2004.

About the Authors

Max Herman began his seven-decade-long music career in 1936 when he joined Joe Haymes, one of the leading musicians of the day, playing first trumpet. During his career, the author played with such legends as Larry Clinton, Bunny Berigan, Gus Arnheim, George Hall, and Bob Crosby. Former CEO of Herman Music and President Emeritus of Musician's Union Local 47, Mr. Herman is now retired and enjoys playing thirty-six holes of golf every week near his home in California.

Floyd Levin has published award-winning articles about jazz throughout the world for over forty years, as well as having authored *Classic Jazz—A Personal View of the Music and the Musicians.* He conducts oral history interviews for the Smithsonian and the Jazz Archive at Tulane University.

Index

122